LOCAL GOVERNMENT ADMINISTRATIVE PRACTICE

'Advance, Britannia!

Long Live the Cause of Freedom!

God save the King!'

Rt. Hon. Winston Churchill, P.C., M.P.,
Prime Minister and First Lord of the Treasury,
Minister of Defence, Lord Warden of the Cinque Ports,
in a broadcast speech to the nation upon the occasion of
Victory in Europe, 8 May 1945

LOCAL GOVERNMENT ADMINISTRATIVE PRACTICE

R.E.C. JEWELL

LL.M.(LOND.)

OF GRAY'S INN, BARRISTER AT LAW

CHARLES KNIGHT & COMPANY LIMITED

LONDON & TONBRIDGE

Published by
Charles Knight & Company Limited
25 New Street Square, Fleet Street, London, EC4A 3JA
and Sovereign Way, Tonbridge, Kent TN9 1RW
A Member of the Benn Group

Printed in Great Britain

ISBN *0 85314–239–4*

Contents

List of Figures

ERRATA

Page 42. Last paragraph should begin:
'Control of development' means dealing with appli
tions for planning permission.

Page 47. First sentence should read:
District councils are both local housing and envir
mental health authorities.

age 53. Third line from the foot should read:
sewer he may be required to construct it so as to fo
part of a general

e 92. Second paragraph, last sentence, 'Control
lso . . .', *belongs to the foot of page 89.*

100. Fig. 2. For '20 London Borough Counc
d '32 London Borough Councils'.

14. Lines 3/4. For 'community council' *read* 'co
ity meeting'.

2. Line 25. For '8p' *read* '0.8p'.

. Line 19. For 'group' *read* 'burgh'.

ERNMENT ADMINISTRATIVE PRACTICE: R. E. C. JEWE

Preface

THE LAST FIVE YEARS, encompassing what might be described as the Extraordinary Parliament of 1970–74, and the even more extraordinary Parliaments ensuing has produced more changes in legislation and the machinery of government than ever before. Huge juggernaut Departments of State have been created. At least two immense and far-reaching statutes have been passed annually, for example those dealing with town and country planning (1971 and 1974), local government reorganization (1972), Scotland and land compensation (1973); and housing (1974). The central government, whilst allowing itself five years for some of its own leisurely tax changes, decreed that local government in England and Wales should be reorganized seventeen months after Royal Assent. Scotland fared no better and was vouchsafed the same period. Local government finance was left gasping for breath, barely beating the eleventh hour. In these circumstances, it is difficult to paint a final picture in some areas and reasonable reviewers will no doubt make allowances for this. The present time of economic recession and near-disaster adds to an author's difficulties, as the situation may well have changed by the time of publication, assuming a firm hand at the tiller and a better spirit in the country at large.

The book aims to develop the syllabuses in Local Government Administrative Practice and Local Government Law for the D.M.A. It should also prove useful to students preparing for the new O.N.C. paper in Public Administration. At degree level the modern approach should assist those reading Government for the B.Sc.(Econ.) Degree and also law students preparing for Constitutional and Administrative Law, both academically and professionally. Legal Executives may also benefit, having regard to the Fellowship Examination in Local Government Law and Practice of their Institute. The book seeks to state the position obtaining at midsummer 1975. R.E.C.J.

Town Hall,
Gateshead
June 1975

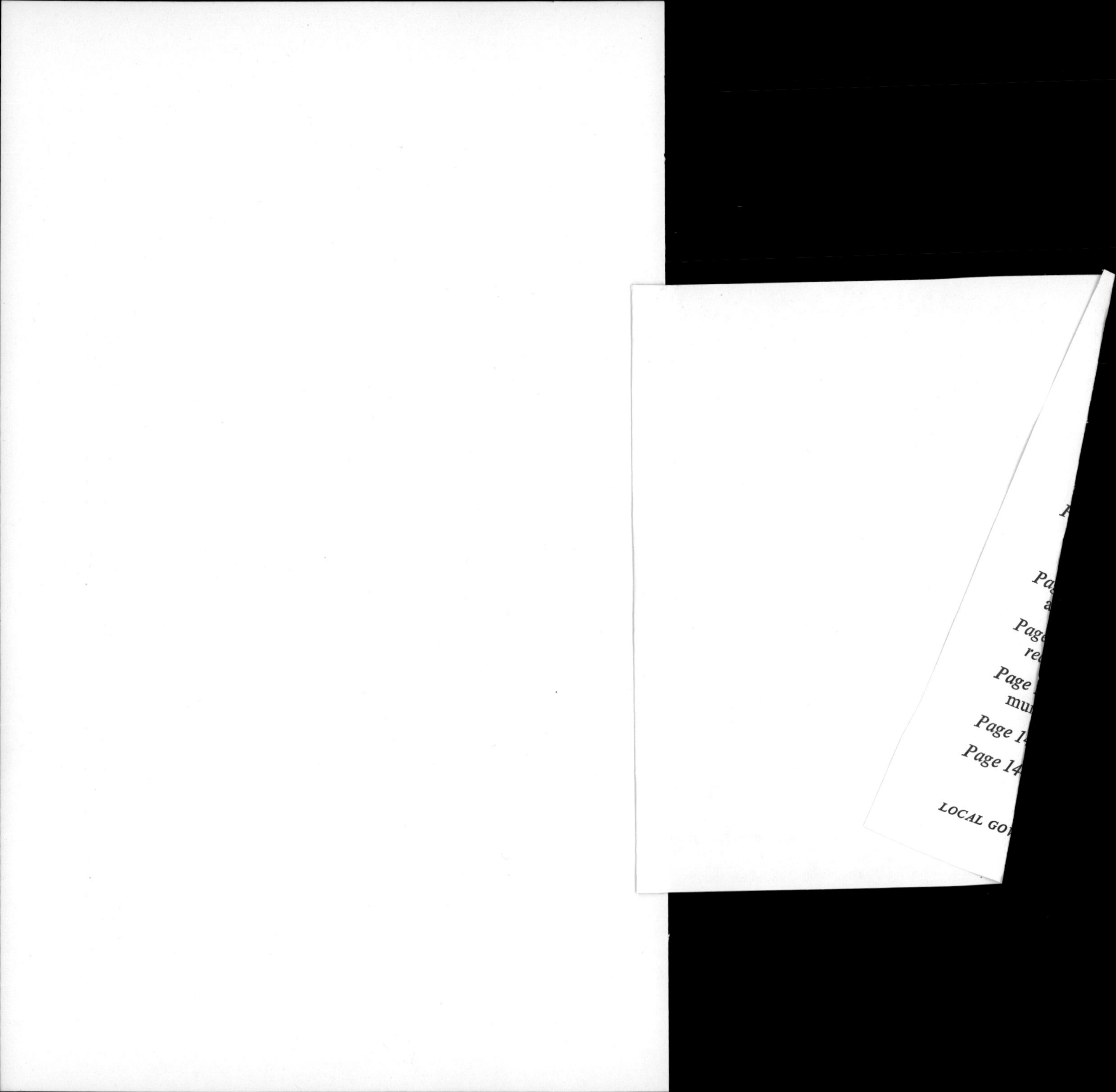

1 THE DEVELOPMENT AND STRUCTURE OF LOCAL GOVERNMENT SINCE 1830

The boroughs and the counties

THE GREAT REFORM ACT of 1832 which enlarged the parliamentary franchise was swiftly followed by the Poor Law Amendment Act, 1834, and the Municipal Corporations Act, 1835. At the beginning of this period reform was in the air, partly owing to the teaching and writing of Jeremy Bentham (1748–1832), the great legal and social philosopher, who propounded the theory of Utilitarianism. According to this the aim should be the achievement of the greatest happiness of the greatest number of people. Curiously enough, Bentham's doctrines have been useful both to the proponents of *laissez-faire* and to the advocates of collectivism. In the latter respect, Bentham was one of the forerunners of the sociological school of jurisprudence which believes that law must have a social purpose. Law is not an arid body of doctrine but a living discipline allied to the concept of liberty and, in a free society, reflecting both the legitimate aspirations of the common people and changing social conditions. In the field of local government, Bentham advocated that the areas in which local authorities were to act should be governed solely by ease of administration. The other main impetus to reform could be discerned in the liberalism of the old Whig Party which resulted initially in the enactment of the Reform Act. By this 'Great Charter of 1832' the rotten boroughs were swept away and many new and rising centres of population received parliamentary representation for the first time.

During the course of centuries, many ancient towns and cities had received Charters of incorporation from the Crown, in the exercise of the royal prerogative. During the reign of Charles II many Charters were called in and reissued in order to ensure Tory and royalist control. A Charter had the effect of incorporating the Mayor, Aldermen and Burgesses of a borough. Some boroughs were also cities as seats of an Archbishop (Canterbury and York) or of a diocesan bishop (e.g. London, Durham and Winchester). There were certain peculiarities about the City of London, as we shall see later: suffice it to say, for the present, that the ancient City Corporation possesses several Charters issued to it by various monarchs. As long ago as the sixteenth century some boroughs provided street lighting, water supply and fire brigades. However, royal intervention and *laissez-faire* doctrines led to inertia and incompetence under municipal oligarchies which were unrepresentative and often corrupt. The Municipal Corporations Act, 1835, vested borough government in the mayor, aldermen and councillors. The corporations were made responsible for the local police force (under the control of borough Watch Committees) and were empowered to make by-laws for good government and prevention of nuisances.

The municipal franchise was based on rateable occupation of property. The Act extinguished ancient trading rights within boroughs and provided for publicity for proceedings of the new councils and for the publication and auditing of accounts. The Act also abolished the old system of electing borough justices by municipal corporations. The law was consolidated in the Municipal Corporations Act, 1882.

In the counties the Crown was represented, as it is today, by a Lord Lieutenant and a Sheriff. However, by 1830 local administration had passed out of their hands to the local justices of the peace. During the previous century the justices in Quarter Sessions had administered the 'county business' after dealing with their judicial work. They were assisted not only by the clerk of the peace but also by such officials as the county surveyor, since the repair and maintenance of certain highways and bridges came within their purview. In addition, the justices had statutory powers over poor law administration, maintenance of public order and licensing of ale houses (the last two matters being not unconnected on occasion!). By the beginning of our period, Parliament had for some time habitually sent bills affecting local administration to the justices for their expert opinion. In this way, as Professor Plucknett points out, 'the opinion of the Knights of the Shires often decided the fate of bills which dealt with local government'. The reform of municipal government in 1835 did not lead to a corresponding alteration in county affairs. The justices of the peace continued more or less undisturbed until 1888, largely owing to their excellent record stretching back to 1361 and even earlier. Their powers even extended to the levying of rates but this was generally accepted despite the nomination of justices of the peace by the Crown.

The growth of *ad hoc* authorities

We have elsewhere described the effect of the Poor Law Amendment Act, 1834. Here Benthamite principles were observed and implemented by Chadwick, a disciple of Bentham. In particular, strong central control was achieved, but we are concerned to note here that, under the Act, local administration was vested in elected boards of guardians, following the union of parishes and workhouses. A purely local administration of the Poor Law was thus supplanted by one in which the local element was subjected to strong central guidance and direction in the guise of the Poor Law Board. Following a report by Chadwick, the Commissioners had investigated sanitary conditions by 1842.

During the early part of the nineteenth century a large number of elected *ad hoc* authorities had been created. An *ad hoc* authority is one formed for a sole specific purpose, in contradistinction to the modern local authority, which is a *general* authority administering several services. Thus at the beginning of our period there were such bodies as highway boards, local boards of health, burial boards, improvement commissioners, boards of guardians, poor law parishes and unions. These were joined later in the century by school boards and school attendance committees.

In 1845 a Royal Commission recommended that water supply, drainage, paving, repairing and cleansing of streets should be carried out in each area by a single authority subject to certain central controls.

The local boards of health were perhaps the genesis of the modern system of local government because the Public Health Act, 1848, which constituted the boards, also enabled a borough council to adopt the Act and become the sanitary authority for its area. Local boards of health were created either at the request of the inhabitants or by order of the Central Board of Health if the death rate was high. It will be recalled that the Act was passed owing to the severe outbreak of cholera in 1847. The boards administered such matters as sewerage, paving, lighting, water supply and burial grounds. Thus although they were *ad hoc* in the generic sense of public health, there was a glimmering of overlapping functions, for example in relation to burial boards. As late as 1883, however, there were eighteen different kinds of rates, elections were held on varying franchises and they were by no means uniform in other respects. The position at this period has been described as 'a chaos of areas, a chaos of franchises, a chaos of authorities and a chaos of rates'.

Although the General Board of Health was dissolved in 1854 Parliament came to realize that central control was too diffuse. Following the Report of a Royal Sanitary Commission the Local Government Board was established in 1871, replacing the Poor Law Board and exercising general supervisory control over local services. The Royal Commission had also indicated that general local authorities were preferable to a proliferation of *ad hoc* authorities. This led to the next great landmark, the Public Health Act, 1875, which is still in force to some extent. This Act definitely designated borough councils as the local authorities for public health matters; in other areas, urban and rural, public health powers were transferred in general to the boards of guardians. The Act codified the law of public health and established urban and rural sanitary districts. Not all urban areas were governed by borough councils, so that outside the boroughs it was necessary to make use of improvement commissioners and local boards of guardians for this purpose. The rural districts comprised the remainder of the poor law unions. The Act of 1875 imposed on urban and rural sanitary authorities definite powers and duties relating to public health and the general provisions of the Act are strictly limited to the discharge of those powers and duties. Thus, in every later Act conferring or imposing on urban district or rural district councils fresh powers or duties (such as housing), new general provisions have had to be enacted. On the other hand, general powers conferred on a borough council by the Municipal Corporation Acts, 1835–82, covered the activities of the corporation acting through its council; but they did not extend to the corporation when it was discharging other specific statutory functions such as public health and housing. In the latter case, authority for action taken must derive from the Public Health Acts or from the Housing Acts.

Nineteenth-century reform

Reform in the counties was ushered in by the Local Government Act, 1888, under which most of the administrative functions of the justices of the peace were transferred to new elected county councils. The most important functions of the new councils initially related to highways. We have here to make a distinction between a geographical county and a administrative county. A large geographical county like Yorkshire was divided into three administrative counties: North Riding, West Riding and East Riding, each with its own county council. Similarly the geographical county of 'famous Lincolnshire' was divided administratively into three parts: Holland-with-Boston, Kesteven and Lindsey, each having a county council. Other examples are furnished by the separate county councils of East and West Sussex. In general, administrative counties were based on the old geographical counties of England and Wales, and a link between the old and the new was maintained in that, in most instances, the clerk of the peace became also clerk of the county council.

The 1888 Act also created county boroughs out of the larger municipalities: in general, a minimum population of 50,000 or more was a prerequisite for this status at that time. Until 1888 all municipal boroughs were the same, both in relation to internal composition and functions. After the Act came into force, they remained the same as regards internal composition; that is, with rare exceptions (e.g. Barnstaple, created a borough by statute), they were all incorporated by Royal Charter, each having a mayor, aldermen and councillors. But a big distinction must be made in respect of their functions, for the county borough council was until 1974 the most powerful unit of local government, exercising all conceivable local government functions. Initially, these were few, but as twentieth-century legislation piled function upon function on local authorities, all were absorbed by the county borough councils administering the larger towns and cities. On the other hand, the non-county borough councils administering the smaller towns exercised only limited functions, because some of the more important functions were and still are the responsibility of the county councils. By contrast, the county borough councils although, of course, remaining physically within the area of the administrative counties in which they were situated, were no longer subordinate to the counties and became completely autonomous units of local government. In some cases old historic cities like Canterbury were able to claim county borough status although their population fell considerably below 50,000. The reason was that they already possessed certain privileges by being 'counties of cities' which meant that they had separate courts of quarter sessions and commissions of the peace and therefore appointed their own sheriffs and coroners. In these circumstances, it was considered appropriate that they should acquire the more powerful status of a county borough.

The Local Government Act, 1894, established smaller authorities operating within the system of county administration. It reclassified urban sanitary authorities other than borough councils as urban district councils and rural sanitary authorities as rural district councils. The smaller, or non-county, borough councils, together with the two types of district council, became responsible for the important allied functions of housing and public health. The 'two-tier' or divided system of local administration was born, contrasting with the unitary county borough system. In both systems, the genesis of the *general* local authority can be discerned, as opposed to the *ad hoc* authority. The 1894 Act also created parish councils in the rural parishes, thus adding a third tier in the rural districts of the counties. If there is no parish council, responsibility devolves upon the parish meeting, which comprises all the local government electors of the parish. The boards of guardians lingered on until 1930.

The twentieth century

The great Public Health Act, 1875, remained the basis of public health law until the enactment of the consolidating Public Health Act, 1936. The close connection of public health and housing is illustrated by the fact that slum clearance powers are given to deal with houses 'unfit for human habitation' and surveys and reports are made by public health inspectors (recently redesignated environmental health officers). There had been some housing legislation in the nineteenth century culminating in the Housing of the Working Classes Act, 1890, which provided for slum clearance and the erection of new houses. Borough councils became housing authorities for these purposes and were joined in 1894 by the new urban and rural district councils. Housing legislation during the twentieth century has been prolific, partly owing to housing shortages caused by wars and speculative development; and partly owing to special problems in relation to rural areas and housing finance. Parliament has enacted six housing statutes during the last decade.

We have already noticed that many important Acts of Parliament were enacted relating to education, casting important duties upon education authorities, notably in 1902 and 1944. A Housing and Town Planning Act was passed in 1909; town and country planning was subsequently divorced from housing, although it is difficult to separate them completely. A lukewarm attempt was made to deal with planning control in an Act of 1932 but it was not until 1947 that the legislature really came to grips with this subject. As in the case of education, planning was transferred to the larger authorities – the county councils and county borough councils – when the importance of the function came to be realized. Occasionally Parliament has taken away functions from local authorities, for example administration of hospitals, national assistance, gas and electricity distribution and rating valuation assessment. The main trend during the century, however, has been to give local authorities new or extended functions requiring local administration of a high order.

Following the Report of the Chelmsford Committee, the Local Government Act, 1933, provided local authorities with a constitutional code in the shape of a framework of general powers. Thus the Act dealt with such matters as the appointment of officers, the provision of office accommodation, the acquisition of land for general purposes, the enactment of by-laws, the promotion of private

Bill legislation and finance. The 1933 Act also made a useful classification of the second-tier authorities in the county system: non-county borough, urban district and rural district councils were described collectively as 'county district councils'. The Local Government Act, 1958, dealt mainly with Finance and Areas.

Local Government Act, 1972

The effect of the Act is to reduce the number of principal local authorities in England and Wales to less than a third of the former number. The new authorities break down as follows:

Counties	
39	Shire Counties in England
8	Shire Counties in Wales
6	Metropolitan Counties in England
53	

Districts	
296	Shire Districts in England
37	Shire Districts in Wales
36	Metropolitan Districts in England
369	

The total number of principal local authorities in England and Wales outside Greater London (G.L.C., City Corporation and thirty-two London Boroughs) is therefore now 422 and there are nearly 20,000 councillors outside London. (Their names are listed in Chapters 7, and a fold-out map included at the end of this book). A detailed account of functions, finance and the background to reorganization will follow in later chapters. The term 'principal local authorities' excludes parish and community councils and meetings.

It is important to grasp that borough councils outside London, urban and rural districts have all disappeared (on 31 March 1974) and were replaced by district councils (on 1 April 1974). Metropolitan areas have been established in the great conurbations – Greater Manchester, Merseyside, South Yorkshire, Tyne and Wear, West Midlands and West Yorkshire – and in these areas the division of functions between county and district is different. Thus the metropolitan district councils are responsible for education and social services as well as for housing and aspects of planning and highways.

The naming of the new authorities was a tremendous exercise in which guidance was given by the Department of the Environment but the decisions were made by local authorities, subject to the approval of the Secretary of State. The temporary machinery of Joint Committees of amalgamating authorities was utilized for this purpose. Elections for the new authorities were held in 1973 so that decisions could be taken on such matters as appointment of staff before becoming fully operational in 1974.

The Act preserves and extends the system of parish council government by means of parish meetings and councils (community meetings and councils in Wales). There are some 8,000 parish councils, varying enormously in size. The few rural borough councils created by the 1958 Act become parish councils. Small free-standing towns which were formerly comprised in small boroughs or urban districts were able to achieve 'successor parish council status' on application to the Secretary of State. The 1894 Act had created parish councils and meetings only in the areas of rural districts and these continue under the 1972 Act despite the abolition of rural district councils. The governmental guidelines are that such towns should be broadly comparable with other small towns or villages having rural parish councils, normally with populations of 10,000 to 20,000; that the proportion of the population of the new district comprised in the town should be high; and that historical factors and the wishes of all pre-existing local authorities should be considered. Many applications have been granted, e.g. Sevenoaks Town (formerly U.D.C.) in Kent. On the other hand, few have been allowed in the metropolitan areas, for example there are only three in South Yorkshire.

Parish councils and meetings are to be congratulated on keeping their place in the new system, with enhanced numbers, powers and duties. In Wales the Secretary of State may direct that there shall be a community council for an existing small borough or urban district and a complete system of communities now covers the whole of Wales, based on the English pattern and with certain differences.

Chartered and statutory authorities: the doctrine of *ultra vires*

We have seen that boroughs outside London achieved their status by means of incorporation by Royal Charter, in the vast majority of cases. All other local authorities are creatures of statute: county councils, district councils, parish councils, parish meetings, community councils. The Common Law origin of a county borough council remained until 1974, despite the acquisition of new functions under Act of Parliament. Originally, there were no county boroughs and they came into existence only since 1888. Despite their more numerous functions, the internal composition and structure of a county borough was exactly the same as that of a non-county borough. In the first instance, the Charter constituted the legal authority for any action taken by a borough council; but with the growth of legislation affecting all types of local authority, a borough council could also be governed and regulated by statutory provision. In the case of a conflict between an Act of Parliament and the common law, the statute prevails. Since a Charter is granted under the exercise of the royal prerogative, which is the residual power of the Crown at Common Law, a statutory requirement would prevail over a provision in the Charter. In the case of the purely statutory local authorities, they must be able to point to an Act of Parliament authorizing action taken.

This brings us to the well-known doctrine of *ultra vires* (beyond the powers). As applied to local government, this means that a local authority can do only those things which it is authorized to do by Act of Parliament. This has been held to cover matters considered to be reasonably incidental to the main purpose and, if necessary, border-line cases can be tested in the Courts. The doctrine applies to all local authorities including borough councils, but in theory the latter can perform acts under the authority of their Charters provided that they are not contrary to a statute. The qualification is necessary owing to the principles stated above, which are based on the doctrine of the sovereignty of Parliament. The Local Government Act, 1972, enables a district council to petition for the grant of a Charter and that special privileges already granted to a borough now included in the district should be preserved. Examples of the latter are power to administer a market or to collect tolls or dues.

The application of the *ultra vires* rules may be illustrated by a case where the Attorney-General, on the relation of a ratepayer, obtained a declaration that Fulham borough council (a metropolitan borough now incorporated in the London Borough of Hammersmith) had acted *ultra vires* by installing a municipal laundry with the latest contrivances operated by officers employed by the council. It was held that this went beyond the powers given in the Baths and Wash-houses Acts, 1846–47. Since then, some local authorities have obtained the necessary powers by local Act of Parliament (*A. G.* v. *Fulham Corporation* [1921] 1 Ch. 440).

Another example of the application of the doctrine is afforded by an Australian case which went on appeal to the Judicial Committee of the Privy Council. The Municipal Council of Sydney had power under a statute to acquire land compulsorily in order to carry out improvements in the city. A compulsory purchase order was made under these powers but the real reason was that an appreciation in value of the area resulting from a street extension scheme should accrue to the local authority which had met the cost of making the new road. The Judicial Committee indicated that a local authority authorized to take land for specific purposes would not be allowed to exercise its powers for different purposes. In other words, the action taken was *ultra vires* the enabling statute (*Municipal Council of Sydney* v. *Campbell* [1925] A.C. 338).

A more recent illustration of the *ultra vires* rule was furnished by the case of the pensioners who were allowed by Birmingham Corporation to travel free on their municipal transport system. A ratepayer tested the legality of this in an action for a declaration and the free travel was held to be *ultra vires* the powers of the Corporation, as no statutory authority existed and the Charter did not provide for such a contingency (*Prescott* v. *Birmingham Corporation* (1955) Ch. 210). An Act of Parliament enacted in the same year gave certain local authorities in the Midlands permissive power to provide free transport for certain classes of persons, including pensioners. These permissive powers were extended to all local authorities in England and Wales by the Travel Concessions Act, 1964, which enables concessions to be made to school children as well as to pensioners. The Transport Act, 1968, enables local authorities to arrange with P.T.E.s for travel concessions for pensioners, blind and disabled persons and these powers are being exercised in many areas today.

An Act passed in 1963 gave a local authority power to incur expenditure *in the interests of its area or inhabitants*, where the expenditure was not otherwise authorized. Such expenditure was limited to the product of a penny rate. Subject to this limitation, this novel statutory provision has provided local authorities with considerable discretion and has enhanced their financial freedom of action since the relevant payments cannot be challenged by the auditor. It is now open to local authorities to incur expenditure on such items as mayoral regalia (which in the past was often provided by public subscription or a generous benefactor) or on 'twinning' arrangements with Continental towns under which civic representatives exchange useful and informative visits. These powers are now contained in the Local Government Act, 1972, which has somewhat widened their scope. Thus section 111 enables local authorities to do anything which is calculated to facilitate, or is conducive or incidental to, the discharge of any of their functions, even if they have no specific statutory power. D.o.E. Circular 121/72 says that this has been included for the avoidance of any doubt which might hamper local initiative.

Local Government Landmarks

1832 Reform Act. Reorganization of 'rotten boroughs' for purpose of the parliamentary franchise
1834 Poor Law Amendment Act – control of poor law authorities
1835 Municipal Corporations Act. New powers given to borough councils (municipal corporations) and regulation of their internal composition and government
1848 Public Health Act. Creation of General Board of Health: control of local boards
1870 Elementary Education Act – local school boards created
1871 Local Government Board created
1875 Public Health Act: borough councils, urban and rural sanitary districts constituted public health authorities
1882 Municipal Corporations Act*
1888 Local Government Act – county councils and county borough councils constituted
1890 Housing of the Working Classes Act
1894 Local Government Act – urban district councils, rural district councils and parish councils created
1902 Education Act – education functions given to local authorities
1909 Housing and Town Planning Act
1918 Education Act: more powers to local authorities
1919 Acquisition of Land (Assessment of Compensation) Act
1925 Rating and Valuation Act
1929 Local Government Act – boards of guardians abolished, de-rating introduced (see Chapter 4)
1932 Town and Country Planning Act
1933 Local Government Act: Code of general powers
1936 Public Health Act.* Housing Act*
1944 Education Act
1947 Town and Country Planning Act
1948 Local Government Act – valuation assessment functions transferred to Inland Revenue (see Chapter 4)
1949 Housing Act
1957 Housing Act*
1958 Local Government Act – Finance, Areas, Delegation
1959 Highways Act.* Town and Country Planning Act. Mental Health Act

1961 Housing Act. Rating and Valuation Act
1962 Town and Country Planning Act*
1964 Housing Act
1965 Control of Office and Industrial Development Act
1966 Local Government Act. Rating Act
1967 General Rate Act.* Civic Amenities Act. Housing Subsidies Act
1968 Rent Act. Town and Country Planning Act
1969 Housing Act. Representation of the People Act
1970 Chronically Sick and Disabled Persons Act. Local Authority Social Services Act
1971 Town and Country Planning Act*
1972 Housing Finance Act. Local Government Act
1973 Land Compensation Act. Water Act. National Health Service Reorganization Act
1974 Local Government Act Housing Act. Town and Country Amenities Act. Rent Act
1975 Housing Rents and Subsidies Act

* Consolidating statutes.

FURTHER READING

Sidney and Beatrice Webb: *The Development of Local Government* 1689–1835, London (Oxford University Press, 1963).
Redlich, J. and Hirst, F. W.: *The History of Local Government in England*, London (Macmillan, 1970).
Rathbone and Pell: Local Administration.

Questions

1. What do you think was the most significant reform of local government in the nineteenth century?
2. How have bodies to represent the 'grass roots' been established in England and Wales?
3. Illustrate the operation of the doctrine of *ultra vires* in local government by reference to case law. Has the doctrine been affected by the Local Government Act, 1972?
4. Outline the changes in the structure of local government effective in 1974.

2 THE INTERNAL ORGANIZATION OF LOCAL AUTHORITIES

Political parties and the machinery of elections and meetings

THE NATIONAL POLITICAL PARTIES nowadays run candidates in local government elections, the general trend having been for the Labour Party to dominate the urban areas and for the Conservatives to hold sway in the rural counties and districts. With the advent of a Liberal revival, this pattern is changing and, at the time of writing, the great city of Liverpool is under Liberal control. For a long time local elections were non-political in the sense that candidates were independent of party influence. Nevertheless, many so-called independent bodies, such as the Independent Ratepayers' Associations, were in reality rarely distinguishable from the Conservative interest; and, until comparatively recently, the Conservatives in London stood as Municipal Reform candidates. Until about ten years ago local government provided a useful training ground for membership of Parliament, but the tendency now is for bright young men to seek parliamentary election without bothering first to serve on a local authority. The alleged decline of local government, coupled perhaps with youthful impatience, is postulated as a reason for this development. Each of the national parties has a local government section or division at their headquarters, with paid officers dealing with such matters as party organization for local elections and research. The Conservatives allocate the last session of their annual party conference to discussion of local government affairs, and hold a separate local government conference in the spring. Some of the longer-serving members of Parliament are also councillors; one or two even manage to serve as Mayor or Lord Mayor of a town or city as well. In general, the same local party agent can service both local and parliamentary elections, although the constituency areas are not necessarily identical.

The same electoral register is used for both parliamentary and local elections. Residence on the qualifying date is accordingly the basis of the franchise. The first two periods of office will be for three years only in the shire districts so that their councillors will not be elected for the full four years until 1979. The non-resident qualifications for voting in local government elections were abolished in 1969.

An adult British or Irish subject can be registered if he is resident in the area and not subject to any legal disability. Special provision is made for service and other absent voters and persons unable to go to the polling station may vote by post.

Candidates in local elections must be adult British or Irish subjects registered as local government electors *or* resident within the area during the whole of the preceding twelve months (the twelve months preceding the date of nomination for election). The Local Authorities (Qualification of Members) Act, 1971, restored the qualifications based on occupation of land or premises and workplace in the area (thus reversing the effect of the Representation of the People Act, 1969, in this respect). These provisions were re-enacted in s. 79 of the Local Government Act, 1972. The main disqualification for election is the holding of any paid office or other place of profit in the gift or disposal of the local authority or of any of its committees. Recorders and coroners are disqualified under these provisions which do not, however, apply to sheriffs, returning officers, mayors and chairmen.

A councillor who resigns cannot be appointed to a paid office under the council until twelve months later even though he receives no remuneration. Other disqualifications include bankruptcy or making a composition with creditors; surcharge in a sum of over £500 and conviction and sentence of imprisonment for not less than three months. This disqualifies if the surcharge or imprisonment was within five years before or since election. Corrupt and illegal practices also disqualify and a court may disqualify in cases of illegal expenditure exceeding £2,000.

The first elections held under the Local Government Act, 1972, were held as follows:

All Counties: 12 April 1973
Metropolitan and Welsh Districts: 10 May 1973
Shire Districts and Parishes in England: 7 June 1973
Community Councils in Wales: 10 March 1974

The term of office of councillors is extended from three years to four. All county and parish councillors will retire together every fourth year (i.e. 1977, 1981, etc.). One-third of metropolitan district councillors will retire in each year between county council elections (i.e. 1974/5/6, 1978/9/80, etc.). Shire districts can elect between all members retiring *en bloc* every fourth year as in the counties or a third retiring in each of the intervening years as in the metropolitan districts. The first two periods of office will be for three years only in the shire districts so that their councillors will not be elected for the full four years until 1979. After the initial elections local government elections each year will be held on the same day, fixed by the Home Secretary, normally the first Thursday in May. Public notice must be given and nominations must be in writing, signed by a proposer, a seconder and eight other local government electors and must contain the candidate's written consent and a statement of his qualifications for election.

The Returning Officer has power to reject a nomination paper only on the grounds that the particulars of the candidate or persons subscribing the paper are not as required by law. He cannot decide any question raised with respect to the disqualification of the candidate. The Returning Officer's decision can be challenged subsequently by means of election petition. Election offences and election petition procedure are the same as for parliamentary elections. No deposit is required of candidates in local elections.

A county council must appoint an officer to be returning officer for the election of county councillors, and a district council must appoint an officer to be returning officer for the election of district, parish or community councillors. Until 1974 this was usually the Clerk, but now it will probably be the Chief Executive or his deputy (if there is one) or the Secretary or Director of Administration. For the first elections the Home Secretary made Orders designating which of the pre-existing authorities forming part of a new authority should appoint the Returning Officer. If the nominations exceed the vacancies, a poll is held by secret ballot. If the nominations correspond to the vacancies, the Returning Officer declares the candidates elected. If the nominations are less than the vacancies he declares those candidates elected; the remainder used to be filled by the retiring councillors who gained the highest number of votes at the previous election. Under the 1972 Act, in such circumstances the Returning Officer must order an election to be held within forty-two days of the day fixed for the original election. This also applies if the poll has been abandoned or countermanded. If for any other reason an election is not held on the appointed day or becomes void, the High Court may order an election to be held. In the case of parish or community council elections being defective the district council may make an appointment to fill a vacancy or cause an election to be held. Casual vacancies normally necessitate by-elections but if one occurs within six months of the end of the term of office the seat remains vacant until the next election, unless more than a third of the seats become vacant, in which case an election is necessary; and a parish or community council fills a casual vacancy by co-option or election. Continuous failure to attend council or committee meetings for six months results in a casual vacancy. The Act makes special provision for casual vacancies occurring in districts subject to annual elections.

Councillors

We have described the procedure for the election of councillors; let us now examine what happens to them once they are elected. First, it is fundamental that all councillors, once elected, are entitled to serve for four years, unless they die or become disqualified. A general election of councillors will be held every four years in the counties and parishes and in some districts. London and the shire districts will eventually conform to the four-year pattern.

In the metropolitan districts one-third of the councillors are elected annually; this is aptly described by Sir William Hart as 'the system of partial renewal', which is also one method in the shire districts. The electoral area of a local authority may be a division or ward or the local government unit itself, owing to the variation in size within all types of unit. There are even some very large parishes: it should be noted that, where there is no parish council, the parish meeting comprising all the local government electors can exercise limited functions. The parish meeting is the only example of direct democracy in the Constitution. Table 1 sets out electoral areas, representation and incidence of elections in relation to the different type of local authority.

A councillor may be elected by his fellow-councillors to be Mayor or Chairman. A councillor may be elected as chairman of the council of a county, district, or parish. Candidates for the office of Mayor or Chairman must be qualified for membership of the council and the election is the first business at the annual meeting immediately following the general election of councillors in May. The expression 'annual meeting' does not mean that it is the only meeting, merely that it is the first meeting in the council year. The person presiding, that is the chairman of the meeting until a Mayor or Chairman has been elected, has a casting vote in the event of a tie. A deputy or Vice-Chairman is appointed from council members.

The aldermanic principle was first introduced in the Municipal Corporations Act, 1835, and was applied to the new county councils by the Local Government Act, 1888. The system of indirect election has been attacked as undemocratic and unrepresentative, to some extent, of the wishes of the electorate. The defence usually advanced for preservation of the system is that it ensures stability and continuity, particularly where political control changes. The Royal Commission on Local Government in England 1966–69 recommen-

Fig. 1 Local Elections

Local Government Area	*Electoral Area*	*Representation*	*Incidence of Elections*
Greater London	Parliamentary Division	One Councillor for each Division	Triennial (all retire *en bloc*) until Home Secretary makes an order
London Borough	Ward	Three Councillors for each Ward usually	As above
Shire (England and Wales) or Metropolitan County (England)	Electoral Division	One Councillor for each Division	Quadrennial (all retire *en bloc*)
Metropolitan District (England)	Ward of District	Number of Councillors for each Ward divisible by three	Annual, except for year of County Council elections
Shire District (England and Wales)	Ward of District	Number of Councillors fixed by Secretary of State on basis of three member or single member Wards	Annual, except for year of County Council elections, or Quadrennial (all retire *en bloc*)
Parish (England)	Parish or Ward of Parish	Fixed by District Council if split into Wards	Quadrennial
Community (Wales)	Community or Ward of Community	As above	As above

ded the abolition of the office of alderman and the 1972 Act has accordingly abolished the office of alderman, except that a principal council may confer the title of honorary aldermen on former councillors and others. The office lingers on in London government until 1976.

Mention should here be made of the vexed question of payment of council members. Reasonable allowances are payable to a mayor or chairman and limited allowances are payable to members in respect of financial loss, travelling and subsistence on 'approved duty'. The scales are revised periodically by the Secretary of State for the Environment but there is general recognition that the system is out of touch with reality. The Wheatley Report on Scotland recommends payment of councillors. The 1972 Act provides for a taxable flat-rate allowance for elected members and a financial loss allowance for co-opted members, and continues the system of travelling and subsistence allowances. An increase was made in subsistence allowances by the Local Government (Allowances to Members) (Amendment) Regulations, 1973 (S.I. 1973 No. 1462).

Finally, it should be noted that a member of a local authority is under a duty to disclose his interest in any contract or other matter before the council or any or its committees, and he must abstain from discussion and voting. This has been another difficult matter, despite the fact that the Minister has power to remove disabilities if the numbers affected are so great as to impede the transaction of business. The original provisions are in the 1933 Act, as amended: the Local Government (Pecuniary Interests) Act, 1964, provides that the duty to disclose and abstain does not apply when the interest is remote or insignificant. Difficulties have arisen in the past in the case of councillors, who were also council house tenants, participating in housing debates and decisions on rent rebate and differential rent schemes. The courts have held that a councillor may be 'interested' in this special sense even if he takes part and votes against his interest; he can still be convicted and fined. In one case a councillor was managing director of a building firm which had not tendered for work to the council for some years; he was nevertheless convicted because he had taken part in a housing committee debate on direct labour building (*Rands* v. *Oldroyd* (1959) 1 Q.B. 204). The courts have interpreted the law very strictly in the past and there is much scope for argument on what exactly is 'remote or insignificant'. Corruption may take place much less openly, as is possible in the field of planning decisions, and it may well be that quite different provisions are necessary to deal with it. If so, the disclosure of interest provisions could be swept away together with the *ultra vires* rule, since they are both remnants of a nineteenth-century approach. However, the old law has been re-enacted in the 1972 Act. In Circular 105/73 (D. o. E.) (202/73 Welsh Office) dispensation was given to members to speak and vote on matters of general housing policy, although they are tenants of unfurnished housing accommodation.

Council meetings and committees

A council must hold an annual meeting and at least three other meetings during the year; in addition, the Mayor or Chairman may call a meeting at any time and may be required to call one on the requisition of members. Nowadays most councils hold more than four meetings a year and in the urban areas monthly meetings are common. Notice of the time and place of a council meeting must be published at the council offices or town hall three clear days beforehand; and a summons to attend specifying the business signed by the proper officer must be sent to each member. Minutes of meetings must be kept and must be signed by the chairman at the next meeting; on payment of five pence, a local government elector can inspect the minutes at the council offices and make copies of extracts. A quorum of members must be present in order to transact business: in general, a quorum is one-quarter of the members.

The committee system is fundamental to local government and chairmen of committees are powerful members of local authorities. Membership of committees is fixed by the council and may include persons who are not members of the authority (except in the case of a committee dealing with finance); but in general the number of co-opted members may not exceed a maximum of one-third of the total membership. A council can remove a member from a committee before his term of office expires. A council can *refer* a specific matter to a committee, which then prepares a report for consideration by the full council. In such a case the recommendation of the committee is not effective until ratified by the council. On the other hand, a council may *delegate* specific matters to a committee: in this case the committee has full executive power so that its decisions are immediately effective. The general rule is that such a committee cannot delegate its executive powers to a sub-committee. A local authority may delegate any of its functions to a committee, except the powers to levy a rate or issue a precept or borrow money. It has been held that the minutes of a planning committee exercising delegated powers are not open to inspection, because they are not technically the minutes of a local authority. On the other hand, the minutes of a committee exercising referred powers, if submitted to the council for approval, are part of the minutes of the council and are therefore open to inspection.

A local authority must appoint certain committees by statute and in general the council may not initiate action except on a recommendation or report of such a committee. A majority of the education committee of a county council or metropolitan district council must be elected members and it must contain members with local knowledge of education. This means that just under half of the members of an education committee may be co-opted, but very few authorities make full use of this provision. A local education authority may delegate powers to an education committee. A county council or metropolitan district council, in its capacity as local social services authority, must appoint a social services committee and can in general only act on its report, save in urgent cases. A majority of the committee must be council members and the committee minutes must be open to inspection. Business may be referred to this committee or functions may be delegated to it.

A power may be conferred directly by statute on a committee: thus outside London the police authority is a committee of the county council known as the police committee. Two-thirds of the members of the committee are council members appointed by the council and one-third are magistrates appointed in accordance with a scheme made by the magistrates courts committee and approved by the Home Secretary.

Local authorities have a general power to make standing orders on such matters as the quorum, proceedings and place of meeting of committees. In 1963 the Ministry of Housing and Local Government issued its second edition of Model Standing Orders (Proceedings and Business of Local Authorities) for the guidance of councils. Fair and accurate reports of meetings of local authorities and their committees are privileged, unless the publication is proved to be made with malice (in which case an action for libel would lie), but this 'qualified privilege' does not extend to meetings to which the public and the press are denied admission. Meetings of local authorities and education committees must be open to the public and this applies where a body resolves itself into committee or where a committee comprises all the members of the local authority. The public and press can be excluded whenever publicity would be prejudicial to the public interest, for example when the council is receiving advice from its officers. The press can demand copies of agenda and supporting documents. The 1972 Act re-enacts these provisions from the pre-existing law.

A further refinement has recently taken place in the district of Basildon, Essex. There, a Policy Executive of ten members submits new policy proposals to the council for approval and it is, in fact, the only committee reporting to the council. All other committees (except leisure and recreation which has twelve members) comprise six members. These committees report to the policy executive and a record of committee decisions is available to councillors. Advisory study groups of members assist the Executive. The prelude to this, under the late town clerk and first town manager, was the abolition of all sub-committees, except for education, and maximum delegation to committees, chairmen and vice-chairmen, with the corollary of greater delegation to officers and the establishment of panels and study groups. The Basildon experiment repays study and certainly deserves success as an exercise in streamlined local democracy.

The new Metropolitan Borough Council of Gateshead provides an example of the application of the Bains Report in the post-reorganisation era. Gateshead has three groups of Committees: Policy and Resources, Personal Services and Technical Services. The Chairman of the Policy and Resources Committee is the Leader of the Council; this Committee allocates resources between the various services and performs the function of a general co-ordinating committee. The Policy and Resources Committee has four sub-committees dealing respectively with finance, personnel, land and common services. The Personal Services group of Committees comprise those dealing with education, social services, housing, libraries, parks and recreation. This group includes the major spending committees providing the personal services directly affecting members of the public. The Technical Services Group of Committees consist of the planning, highways, public protection and environmental health Committees.

The Council and its Committees meet monthly during the day, except in August. The Chief Executive at Gateshead is Secretary to the Council and as such has direct control of the administrative sections of the department of the Director of Legal Services. The Chief Executive is Chairman of the Management Team of Chief Officers which meets weekly, except in August. The Director of Finance is the Deputy Chief Executive, although the Director of Legal Services is responsible for the Council's central administration under the direction of the Chief Executive. There are a number of officers' working groups whose main purposes are to ensure that corporate advice is given to committees, and that the activities of the various departments are properly co-ordinated in carrying out policy.

The Chief Officers normally reporting to the Housing Committee, for example, would be the Chief Executive; the Directors of Legal Services, Housing, Architectural Services, Engineering Services, Public Works and Planning; and the Chief Environmental Health Officer. There is also a Working Group of third-tier officers on Inter-Departmental Co-ordination.

The 1972 Act abolishes, with certain exceptions, statutory requirements to establish committees. It is interesting that the exceptions, all relate to services not controlled by the Department of the Environment – education, social services and police. Having established this revolutionary principle (with limitations) the Secretary of State, in consultation with the local authority associations, set up a Study Group of Local Authority Management Structures (the Bains Committee), which reported in August 1972. Their main recommendation on committee structure was that there should be a Policy and Resources Committee with four sub-committees for Finance, Personnel, Land and Performance Review (this means O and M or work study or Lamsachistical refinements thereof). The statutory and other necessary committees can be constructed round this vital Committee. which virtually replaces the old Finance, General Purposes and Establishment Committees. It is important to speak the correct jargon; thus you will find highways under the rubric of 'transportation' (nothing to do with Australia!) and the 'in-word' for planning is now 'development'. What is left of public health becomes environmental health, whilst consumer protection, leisure and amenity services are rightly of increasing importance. The Bains Report was followed by the Ogden Report for Water Reorganization and the Paterson Report for Scotland.

Chief officers and the local government service

A local authority has a general power to appoint such officers as it thinks necessary. Under the 1933 Act, the clerk, treasurer and surveyor had to be 'fit' persons; presumably this meant something more than mere physical fitness, but the term is nowhere defined. In some cases a minimum standard of professional and technical qualifications is ensured, as in the case of chief fire officers under regulations made by the Home Secretary, who must approve the appointment of a chief constable. The Secretaries of State for Education and Science and for Social Services have power to veto the appointments respectively of chief education officers and directors of social services. This power was used by the Secretary of State for

Social Services in 1973 in the case of a Birmingham appointment. The 1972 Act repeals statutory requirements to appoint specified officers, with certain exceptions (these include chief education officers, directors of social services, chief officers and other members of fire brigades and inspectors of weights and measures). Again, the influence of the other government departments can be discerned. However, even the Department of the Environment found it necessary to provide specifically for the appointment of electoral registration officers, officers to have responsibility for the administration of financial affairs (so much simpler than a mere Treasurer!) and national parks officers. As clerks, treasurers and surveyors need no longer be appointed the device of the 'proper officer' has emerged to embody the spirit, and perhaps even the substances of these erstwhile officers. Thus plans are now deposited with the proper officer instead of the clerk – such is progress! Actually, it is amazing what the proper officer can do. He can act as parish trustee, has functions with respect to ordnance survey, deposit and authentication of documents, and he can keep the roll of freemen (if there are any left!) – and these are only examples.

The government was again rescued by the Bains Report, which recommended that each authority should appoint a Chief Executive to act as leader of the officers and principal adviser to the council on general policy matters. The post should be open to officers of any discipline and its occupant free of specific departmental responsibilities. Each authority should establish a Management Team of Principal Chief Officers responsible for plans, programmes and co-ordination of their implementation. Departmental structure should be based on corporate management with multi-disciplinary working groups of officers and area officers in the larger authorities.

The new local authorities have made valiant attempts to carry out the recommendations of the Bains Report. Many have made use of Appendix H (terms of reference for a policy and resources committee) and Appendix J (Job Specification for a Chief Executive). Some have appointed the pure and orthodox non-departmental 'think tank' chief executive; others have combined the post with that of Clerk or Secretary; yet others, very naughty, have appointed Deputy Chief Executives who are Clerks/Secretaries or Directors of Administration and even Deputy Secretaries! Five districts in one shire county produced five variations:

1. Chief Executive
   District/City Treasurer
   Director of Works

Chief City Planning Officer
Director of Housing
Amenities and Recreation Officer

2. Chief Executive
Secretary
Treasurer
Chief Technical Officer (including Planning)
Chief Environmental Health Officer
Chief Housing Officer

3. Chief Executive
Secretary
Treasurer
Chief Technical Officer
Chief Planning Officer
Chief Housing Officer
Chief Environmental Health Officer

4. Chief Executive
Secretary
Director of Finance
Director of Planning and Technical Services
Director of Environmental Health Services
Director of Housing

5. Chief Executive and Clerk
Housing Officer
Planning Officer
Treasurer
Engineer and Surveyor
Environmental Health Officer
Secretary

In circular 111/73 (Welsh Office 204/73) D. o. E. say (para. 12): 'It is important that the authority under which an officer acts should always be easily identifiable. This applies, of course, whether the action is required to be taken by a 'proper officer' or not. It is suggested that any subscription to a document should show the title of the officer signing it and his authority to act, for example:

....
Chief Executive
(The officer appointed for this purpose.)'

If an officer has an interest in any contract he must disclose this fact in writing unless it is remote or insignificant; and he must not accept any fee or reward other than his remuneration. An officer must account for money or property committed to his charge. An authority can ratify a decision made by an officer if it is *intra vires*. A local authority is now bound by a contract entered into on its behalf by a duly authorized officer (Corporate Bodies Contracts Act, 1960).

Full-time local government officers must contribute to a superannuation scheme and may transfer from one authority to another without detriment to their rights. Officers hold office on such reasonable terms and conditions including remuneration, as the appointing authority thinks fit. Nowadays, however, local authorities are bound by national agreements on pay and conditions of service.

FURTHER READING

Long, Joyce and Norton, Alan: *Setting Up the New Authorities*, London (Charles Knight, 1972).

The New Local Authorities: management and structure, London, H.M.S.O., 1972 (the Bains Report).

Questions

1. 'Politics should be kept out of local government.' Do you agree?
2. Describe the arrangements for electoral areas, representation and incidence of elections in the principal local authorities in England (outside London) and Wales.
3. Examine the organization and administration of *one* local government service with particular reference to:
   (a) its place in the committee structure of the council;
   (b) the respective roles of its elected members and officers;
   (c) the effects upon it of central control;
   (d) the impact of public opinion.
4. What should be the principal purposes of the Policy and Resources Committee of a local authority?
5. How are the duties of the traditional clerk or town clerk now discharged?

3 THE FUNCTIONS OF LOCAL AUTHORITIES

THE FUNCTIONS OF LOCAL AUTHORITIES are many and varied and it is not possible to give a detailed account in a work of this nature. An outline of four of the most important groups of functions follows, but it should be borne in mind that special provisions apply to Greater London. This account therefore relates to local authorities in England (outside London) and Wales.

I Education and Social Services

EDUCATION

The modern system of public education in this country derives from the war-time Education Act, 1944. The local education authorities are now shire county councils, metropolitan district councils and joint education boards; there is provision for the establishment of joint education committees. A Joint Education Board is a corporate body which can be formed to administer education over a wider area and it can hold land, borrow money and precept upon its constituent authorities. A Joint Committee, on the other hand, has no corporate status, no independent financial powers and cannot hold property; its constitution is contained in an agreement between the appointing authorities.

Local education authorities must provide primary, secondary and further education. Authority exists in the 1944 Act to raise the upper limit of the compulsory school age to sixteen, and this has at last been done by Ministerial Order effective in 1973. Preparations for ROSLA (raising of the school-leaving age) were made well in advance of its operation and extra finance was allocated to secondary schools to cope with it. As Chairman of the Governors of an inner London comprehensive school for three years, the writer's experience was that the project has been successfully achieved. A small disgruntled minority exists, of course, but Lord Longford's resignation from the Labour government on this issue has been thoroughly vindicated. If we had always waited for everyone to be ready, the school-leaving age would still be 12. Children under 16 can now have work experience as part of their education. In general, pupils are to be educated in accordance with the wishes of their parents and their different ages, abilities and aptitudes; and no fees must be charged. It is the duty of parents to send their children to school or to make other satisfactory provision; this can be enforced by means of school attendance orders and by prosecution in the magistrates' courts.

County schools are those established by a present or former authority; voluntary schools are maintained by a local education authority but were originally established by a religious or charitable foundation. Managers or Governors of a county school are appointed by the local education authority from members of political parties in the area; in the case of voluntary schools, a proportion are 'foundation' managers or governors. In the case of voluntary aided schools, governors or managers are responsible for outstanding liabilities, necessary alterations to buildings, and external repairs; the authority is responsible for internal, playground and playing field repairs, maintenance expenses and repairs necessitated by ancillary use of the premises (for example, as an evening institute for further education). Managers or governors receive a direct grant from the Minister of 80 per cent of the cost of alterations and repairs. In the case of special agreement schools, grants have been made by the authority and the position of managers and governors is similar to those of aided schools.

The managers or governors of voluntary controlled schools merely provide the premises; the authority is fully responsible for maintenance, alteration and repair. In county controlled and special agreement schools, the authority can appoint or dismiss teachers except that in the voluntary schools managers or governors can control appointment or dismissal of 'reserved teachers' responsible for religious instruction. Teachers in voluntary aided schools are appointed by managers or governors within limits set by the authority, which can veto appointment or require dismissal, other than dismissal of 'reserved teachers' on religious grounds. In county schools the day begins with Assembly, comprising undenominational collective worship from which a parent is free to withdraw his child. Christian teaching is provided in accordance with an agreed syllabus prepared by representatives of the various churches and teachers. In aided and special agreement schools the instruction is normally in accordance with the trust deed or former practice. In some areas county school governors now include representatives of a university, teaching staff and parents. Voluntary school governors and managers are appointed by the educational or religious foundation which originally provided the school.

In general, teachers employed by local education authorities must be recognized as 'qualified' by the Secretary of State. The majority of teachers who have completed their training in and since 1963 have undertaken a three-year course. Considerable progress has been made in recent years in the provision of training for mature students. Teachers' training colleges had been established, maintained and governed by local education authorities or voluntary bodies; and university Institutes of Education had been associated with the maintenance of academic standards. The Robbins Report on Higher Education (1963) recommended fundamental changes to bring the colleges under the control of university Schools of Education. In 1964, the government decided to leave the colleges under local or voluntary control, but closer academic links with the universities were to be encouraged. They were renamed Colleges of Education, as suggested by the Robbins Report.

Control of the colleges is divided between local education authorities and governors, as in the case of secondary schools. A significant difference, however, is that the governors of a college of education include a substantial proportion of the teaching staff. The Education (No. 2) Act, 1968, provides that the governing bodies have greater autonomy and they are no longer sub-committees of the local education authority. The staff of polytechnics are now eligible for membership of the local authority by whom they are employed.

The Secretary of State has designated some thirty polytechnics in England and Wales as the main higher education centres within the further education system.

The Open University, based on the concept of the 'University of the Air' has now been given its Charter. It is designed to help part-time and mature students who are unable, for one reason or another, to undertake full-time study. This venture has proved very popular.

The remuneration of teachers until 1945 was dealt with by a Burnham Committee, which was named after its first chairman. Following the enactment of the 1944 Act, the Minister appointed a new Burnham Committee with an independent chairman, twenty-six representatives of the authorities and twenty-six representatives of the teachers. The Committee's duty was to submit agreed salary scales to the Minister for his approval. The Minister could not compel negotiations nor could he modify the scales; his only course was to reject them if he disapproved. This state of affairs was unsatisfactory and in 1963 new scales had to be introduced by statute. Finally, the Remuneration of Teachers Act, 1965, set up committees under an independent chairman and including representatives of the Secretary of State. The Act provides for arbitration in default of agreement and for orders made under it to have retrospective effect. All teachers in maintained schools are paid by the local education authority and their conditions of service are negotiated between the local authority associations and the teachers' organizations, of which the National Union of Teachers is the most prominent.

Special provision must be made for handicapped children (but mentally handicapped children are no longer classified as unsuitable for education at school) and for further education of persons over compulsory school age. Maintained special schools now have governing bodies which are not sub-committees of the local education committee. Authorities must arrange free transport or pay reasonable expenses to a pupil if his school is not within 'walking distance' of his home (over three miles for children over 8; over two miles for children under 8). The controversial Education (Milk) Act, 1971, prevented local education authorities from supplying milk (except on medical grounds) to pupils other than those attending primary or special schools.

Under the Public Libraries and Museums Act, 1964, as amended, library facilities must be provided by the councils of shire counties and metropolitan districts. The 1972 Act enables the Secretary of State for Education to constitute district councils in Wales library authorities but all applications have been rejected, even in the case of the city of Cardiff. The reason is believed to be the adverse effect which such an order would have on the county library service. No doubt the unhappy fragmentation of the old county of Glamorgan played its part in this no less unfortunate decision. Joint Boards may be constituted and charges may be made for failure to return books within due time. The 1964 Act enables local authorities to provide and maintain museums and art galleries.

SOCIAL SERVICES

Although the National Health Service Act, 1946, transferred hospitals to Hospital Boards, the local authorities remained responsible for the personal health services. The authorities had to submit proposals under the Act to the Minister of Health for health centres, maternity and child welfare, midwifery, health visiting and home nursing, vaccination and immunization, ambulances, prevention of illness and after-care and domestic help. Owing to financial stringency few health centres have been established; the aim is to co-ordinate medical, dental and pharmaceutical services under one roof in order to provide a better service to the public.

Local welfare authorities submitted schemes of administration to the Minister of Health for modification or approval. Welfare authorities provided residential accommodation for the aged and infirm and for persons in urgent need of temporary accommodation. There was power to inspect homes for the aged, disabled or mentally disordered. Authorities must promote the welfare of blind, deaf, physically handicapped and mentally disordered persons and can use voluntary agencies for these purposes. Personal health and welfare powers have been supplemented by the Mental Health Act, 1959, in relation to mentally disordered persons.

County councils and county borough councils administered the Children Acts, 1948–58, under the general guidance of the Home Secretary. They had a duty to take into care any child under 17 who is an orphan or who has been abandoned or lost or whose parents or guardians cannot provide for him. An authority may by resolution assume parental rights and a court may commit a child to the care of a local authority. Such children may be boarded out in foster homes or placed in homes run by the authority. There is provision for the parents to contribute towards maintenance of their children.

The Children and Young Persons Act, 1963, provided, for the first time, that local children's authorities have a duty to *prevent* or diminish the need to receive children into care. This power enabled such a local authority to make grants to individual families. It is well-known that prevention is better than cure and many organizations concerned with child care, such as the Association of Children's Officers, had long been pressing for such a provision.

The main conclusion of the Seebohm Report was that all major authorities should have a unified social services department under a chief officer who would have no other duties and would report to a separate social services committee. This would embrace services relating to children, the aged, the disabled, the handicapped and some social services discharged in health (e.g. home help, meals on wheels), education (e.g. school care committees) and housing (e.g. housing estate management and rent collection) departments. The Report also called for more manpower, more extensive training, improved buildings and research. The chief officer should not be subordinate to any other departmental head and should work as a member of a team under the leadership of the clerk. He should be a trained social worker and a gifted administrator. The Secretary of State for Social Services should be involved in his selection. There should be close liaison between the departments and the Supplementary Benefits Commission. The contribution made by voluntary bodies was also recognized by the Seebohm Committee. The unification should provide an effective family service. Housing should be discharged by the same tier as local health, education and welfare. The aim should be to provide 'one door on which to knock'. The Local Government Grants (Social Need) Act, 1969, enables a new specific grant to be paid to local authorities on account of expenditure which, in the opinion of the Secretary of State, is incurred in respect of 'special social need' in urban areas.

The Green Paper on the National Health Service recommended that some seven hundred local health authorities should be replaced by forty area health boards, which would inherit the functions of executive councils, R.H.B.s, H.M.C.s and boards of hospital governors. These proposals were very unpopular in local government circles. A consensus in favour of a two-tier solution appeared to be emerging, with Regional authorities as the first tier and district executives based on districts served by one or more hospitals as the second tier. Election should be the basis of representation on these bodies.

The Health Services and Public Health Act, 1968, extended powers relating to provision of midwives and home helps and enabled charges to be made and local health authorities to provide and to charge for residential accommodation. The authorities must keep a register of premises where children are looked after under the Nursery and Child Minders Regulation Act, 1948. Accommodation can now be provided under the National Assistance Acts in premises managed by a voluntary body and local authorities have wide powers to promote the welfare of old people. Statutory provisions on notifiable diseases are extended (e.g. a family doctor must notify the community physician if he suspects that his patient is suffering from cholera or smallpox).

It should be realized that the foregoing account is a historical background to the drastic reorganizations effected by the Local Authority Social Services Act, 1970, the Chronically Sick and Disabled Persons Act, 1970, and the National Health Service Reorganization Act, 1973. Dealing with the 1970 statutes first (they both received Royal Assent on the same day) local authorities were required to establish social service committees to administer the child care, personal health and welfare functions described above. To this extent, Seebohm was implemented but the housing recommendations were largely ignored. The local social services authorities under the Local Government Act, 1972, are now the shire county councils, metropolitan district councils and London borough councils, and as the two last types of authority are also responsible for housing Seebohm has at least come into its own in the conurbations. Provision is made for the establishment of joint social services committees by two or more local authorities. Local social service authorities were also required to appoint a director of social services and the Secretary of State may make regulations prescribing the requisite qualifications; he also has the power of veto. The statutory requirement to appoint a children's officer was abolished. The two councils established in 1962 for Health Visiting and Social Work Training were renamed the Council for the Education and Training of Health Visitors and the Central Council for Education and Training in Social Work. The second 1970 statute placed duties on social services and housing authorities to assist the chronically sick and disabled by provision of welfare services and housing accommodation. Provision is made for co-option of such persons on to local authority committees and consumer councils of public corporations. This was originally a private member's Bill and affords a good example of much-needed legislation deriving from a back-bench M.P. Except for the changes in administering authorities, the Chronically Sick and Disabled Persons Act was unaffected by subsequent legislation. The National Health Service Reorganization Act, 1973, transferred all personal health functions except those referred to social services committees (care of mothers and children; home helps) from local authorities to the Secretary of State acting through Regional Health Authorities. Provision was therefore made for transfer of property and staff, including some staff employed by local *public* health authorities (who were thus attacked by two statutes simultaneously – N.H.S. Reorganization and Water). In these circumstances the Medical Officer of Health had no chance and also disappeared from the scene.

Schemes or regional plans made by a children's regional planning committee are continued in force by the 1972 Act. (Britain's first children's centre was opened in Islington in 1973 as the National Children's Bureau.) The 1973 Act requires local authorities to give social work support to the reorganized health service. Hospital social workers are now therefore employed by the local authorities and made available to hospitals and other health establishments. This is subject to safeguards for staff in the conditions and location of their work. The reason for this arrangement is that local authorities are by far the major employer of social workers and provide a service on a much wider basis than the hospital service. Medical and dental treatment under the school health service has also been transferred to the N.H.S., this time from local education authorities. The Health Education Council has been expanded and will continue its advisory work.

II Town and Country Planning

Parliament first turned its attention to this subject in the Housing and Town Planning Act, 1909, which enabled borough and urban district councils to make town planning schemes. A similar Act of 1919 required local authorities to prepare schemes and in 1925 they were given extended powers. The Local Government Act, 1929, brought the county councils into the picture for the first time and empowered them to act jointly with other authorities for this purpose. The Town and Country Planning Act, 1932, required county borough and county district councils to make planning schemes and authorized the appointment of joint committees. The local planning authorities passed resolutions to prepare schemes, which became effective when approved by the Minister of Health (the Minister then in charge of local government), who could also make interim development orders. Much of the war-time legislation was incorporated in the Town and Country Planning Act, 1947, which provided the basis of all subsequent planning law, which was consolidated in 1962 and 1971.

Local planning authorities are county councils for county areas, district councils for districts and Joint Boards. The 1947 Act required the preparation of development plans, subject to review at five-yearly intervals. The plans define sites and allocate areas of land for specific uses (residential, commercial, industrial, etc.). There was also a very wide power to *designate* as subject to compulsory acquisition land allocated by the plan for *any* of the functions of *any* Minister, local authority or statutory undertaker. This was the widest power of compulsory purchase contained in any statute; and it applies also to land in a comprehensive development area, that is, an area which is to be replanned on a large scale owing to re-location of population or industry or replacement of open spaces. The wording has been changed but the meaning is the same (T.C.P.A. 1971, L.G.A. 1972). If a compulsory purchase order is made in respect of designated land, the Mniister may disregard any objection which amounts in substance to an objection to the provisions of the plan defining the proposed use of the land. The reason for this is that objectors had their opportunity on the occasion of the last review of the plan. An owner-occupier of land allocated for a particular use can serve a purchase notice on the local authority if its rateable value does not exceed £2,250 and provided that he can prove that the designation has caused 'blight' to settle on the land. This means that he has been unable to sell property except at a price substantially lower than current market value. The local authority may serve a counter-notice denying this and the matter is then settled by the Lands Tribunal. The blight provisions have been considerably enlarged by the Land Compensation Act, 1973 (see Chapter 5). A local authority may carry out development or grant building leases to private developers. It must, however, secure alternative accommodation in advance of displacing residents. The 1968 Act provided that local planning authorities shall make substantive plans for strategic planning and allows them also to make local plans. The Town and Country Planning Act, 1971, took this a stage further by requiring county councils to prepare structure plans (including 'action areas' for comprehensive development) for their areas; and the second-tier authorities, now district councils, must prepare local plans, in both cases subject to approval by the Secretary of State. An examination in public on structure plans has replaced the public inquiry based on the formal hearing of objections. There is now no absolute right on the part of an objector or local planning authority to be heard, although the Secretary of State has a duty to consider all objections. (See *Structure Plans: the Examination in Public,* H.M.S.O., 1973, to which is annexed a specimen form for objections or representations (see also D. o. E. circulars 36 and 74/73)). Publicity material has also been issued by the two Departments. Local planning authorities can now institute joint surveys, prepare joint reports and structure plans for combined areas; such plans can be withdrawn before approval.

In the case of local plans, the county must first prepare a development plan scheme after consultation with its districts, which then prepare their local plans, including one for each action area (comprehensive development in urban areas). The certificate of the county planning authority that the local plan conforms generally to the structure plans is required before a local plan can be effective. As with structure plans, the local planning authority must consult the public and give proper consideration to their views. A local inquiry before an inspector hears objections but local plans are confirmed by the local authority. D. o. E. have set in train a new survey of derelict and despoiled land related to the new districts.

'Control of development' means new structure and local plans negotiations were made in 1974 dealing with applications for planning permission. The Act defines development as:

(1) the carrying out of building, engineering, mining or other operations in, on, over or under land; or
(2) the making of any material change in the use of buildings or other land.

Some years ago the Ministry, presumably trying to be helpful, indicated that a material change of use is a change of use which is substantial. However, the Act does give examples, such as the use as two or more dwellings of a building previously used as a single dwelling; and the formation or layout of means of access to a highway. Again, certain operations and uses are declared not to be development, such as the use of existing buildings or land within the ground (technically the curtilage) used for the comfortable enjoyment of a dwelling-house; or the use of land or buildings for the purposes of agriculture or forestry. Application may be made to the local planning authority to determine whether a proposed operation or change of use constitutes development. The current authority is the T.C.P. General Development Order, 1973 (S.I. 1973 No. 31).

An applicant for planning permission need not be the landowner but, if he is not, he must notify all owners or publish a notice in the local press; and notice must be given to any agricultural tenants. The law was changed in this respect in 1959 because prospective purchasers were seeking planning permission without the knowledge of landowners; and agricultural tenants need special protection owing to their general insecurity of tenure. An authority must not deal with 'bad neighbour development' (e.g. construction of public conveniences) until twenty-one days after advertisement in the local press. 'Outline planning permission' can settle an application in principle, leaving points of detail to be filled in later: the developer can then go ahead with siting and design before submission of final plans. Applications are considered by district councils which can, however, refer them to county councils for decision.

A local planning authority may grant or refuse planning permission and may attach conditions or limitations on its duration. Permission may be granted for development which is contrary to the development plan so long as it is not a substantial departure and does not injuriously affect the amenity of adjoining land. Appeal lies to the Minister within twenty-eight days and his decision can be challenged within six weeks only on the grounds that it is *ultra vires* or that the applicant's interest has been substantially prejudiced by non-compliance with a statutory requirement (the 'challenge procedure'). The Minister may 'call in' applications for his initial decision. The challenge procedure can be used in the case of development plans (i.e. structure, local or action area plans).

An authority may not grant permission to erect or enlarge an industrial building over a certain limit unless the Department of Industry issues an industrial development certificate. The Control of Office and Industrial Development Act, 1965 enabled the Minister to reduce the limit, which he has done in certain areas, and also introduced control of office building. An office development permit must now similarly be obtained before planning permission can be granted in London and the Home Counties but this so-called control hardly seems very effective or is little used. Costly compensation for refusal or revocation of planning permission is of course a factor in some cases of expensive industrial or office development. Under the Industrial Development Act, 1966, an industrial development certificate attaches to the *project*, not to the *land*.

There are now stringent provisions for the enforcement of planning control. A local planning authority may serve on the owner and occupier of land an enforcement notice specifying the alleged contravention and the action to be taken to put the matter right. It is important that the notice should be served within four years of the contravention and that it should specify a period of not less than twenty-eight days at the end of which it takes effect *and* a period of compliance. An enforcement notice which does not specify *both* periods is null and void and can be set aside in the courts. Appeal lies on several specified grounds to the Minister and from him to the High Court. When an enforcement notice has become effective, the authority may enter the land and do any necessary work, charging the owner with the cost. Fines may be imposed and an enforcement notice is not now discharged by compliance. Until 1960 it was so discharged and there were cases of individuals moving structures from field to field, causing the local authority to invoke the enforcement procedure all over again after each move. The only way to deal with such evasions and flouting of the law was by means of an injunction issuing from the High Court but the strengthened enforcement procedure has made this unnecessary.

Certain appeals are now decided by inspectors instead of by the Secretary of State (e.g. tree preservation orders, refusal of established use certificate, control of listed buildings, building operations, most uses of land and certain appeals against enforcement notices).

A material change in use can be caught by an Enforcement Notice at any time provided the change occurred after the end of 1963. But if the material change is to use as a single dwelling-house the development will be safe whenever it occurred. Building operations still enjoy the protection of the four-year rule.

Penalties for breach of an enforcement notice have been increased (in general from £100 to £400). A stop notice can now be served following an enforcement notice to prevent breach of planning control during the twenty-eight-day period between its service and coming into operation. This only applies to building operations (not to material change of use) and there is provision for compensation.

The 1968 Act also gives more extensive powers for conservation of buildings of special architectural or historic interest. The classic *raison d'être* of planning law is the preservation of local amenities in accordance with a central direction of policy laid down by Parliament. To this end, local planning authorities may make tree preservation orders and building preservation orders. In the former case, there is overlapping with the powers of the Forestry Commission. The latter orders relate to buildings of special architectural or historic interest; the Ministry has compiled lists of such buildings and prima facie a listed building should be protected. The challenge procedure applies to these powers.

The Civic Amenities Act, 1967, enabled local planning authorities to designate 'conservation areas' of special architectural or historic interest and for the preservation and enhancement of their character and appearance. At least six months' notice must now be given of works affecting listed buildings and the penalties for contravention of a building preservation order are increased. The Act also provides for more adequate provision in respect of the preservation, planting and replacement of trees. This has been supplemented by the Town and Country Planning (Amendment) Act, 1972, which controls the demolition of listed buildings (after several had been razed to the ground by unscrupulous developers) and provides grants for enhancement of conservation areas of outstanding interest. The Town and Country Amenities Act, 1974, strengthens the law in this field, particularly in relation to conservation areas and areas of special control. Local authorities have been encouraged to enter schemes which might be eligible for an award by the Council of Europe in European Architectural Heritage Year, 1975. Pilot studies have been undertaken in Bath, Chester, Chichester, King's Lynn and York.

Advertisement Regulations control the display of advertisements in the interests of amenity and safety; there are more stringent checks in areas of special control but in general they must be clean, tidy and safe, road safety requirements nowadays being an important factor. Where local amenity is seriously injured by the condition of any garden, vacant site or other open land, an abatement notice may be served on the owner and occupier. Appeal lies to the local magistrates court.

The Countryside Act, 1967, redesignated the National Parks Commission as the Countryside Commission, responsible for the promotion of public enjoyment of the countryside. The Act provides for the creation of Country Parks on the coast and in the countryside, in order to relieve pressure on the National Parks. Exchequer grants to National Parks and areas of outstanding natural beauty have been continued and extended to include the Country Parks, amenity tree planting and increased public access to open country. Local authorities are given extended powers to provide amenities in Country Parks, camping and picnic sites. Under the Local Government Act, 1972, county councils must establish National Parks Committees and in multi-county parks such committees are to be set up by agreement or jointly by the counties concerned. New Joint Planning Boards have been created for the Lake District and Peak District. Two-thirds of the members of the committees will be appointed by the counties, one-third by the Secretary of State.

The Commons Registration Act, 1965, provides for the registration of common land and of village greens. The purpose of the Act is to establish what land in England and Wales is common or a town or village green, what rights of common exist and to place on record who claims ownership of the land. Commons Commissioners appointed by the Lord Chancellor from the legal profession resolve disputes and they may be assisted by technical assessors. Registers are open to public inspection and adequate publicity and information must be given by the local registration authorities. The Act does not affect rights of access to commons, nor does it extend to land that forms part of a highway. The New Forest, Epping Forest and the Forest of Dean are exempted from registration.

Compensation for compulsory acquisition is payable under the Land Compensation Act, 1961, and is based on the current market value of the land, assuming a willing purchaser and a willing vendor. Valuers must take into account the existing use of the land and planning permissions already in force. The Lands Tribunal is available to decide disputes on the correct amount of compensation. Where permission has been refused or is conditional and the owner claims that his land is useless to him in its existing state, he can serve a purchase notice on the district council. If the Minister confirms the notice it has the same effect as a compulsory purchase order. Compensation for depreciation of value of interests in land is now governed by the Land Compensation Act, 1973.

Finally, it should be noted that the Town Development Act, 1952, authorizes development in the shape of the expansion of existing towns in order to decentralize population and industry. The 'exporting' local authority sends its 'overspill' population to the 'receiving' local authority and pays to the latter a contribution equal to the central subsidy.

III Housing and environmental health

HOUSING

District councils are both local housing environmental and health authorities. The close historical connection between the two services can be discerned in the procedure for slum clearance. Environmental health officers must inspect houses in their areas and make an official representation to the local housing authority if of the opinion that a house is unfit for human habitation. The Housing Act, 1957, re-enacting the old law, postulates ten standards of fitness: state of repair; stability; freedom from damp; internal arrangements; natural lighting; ventilation; water supply; drainage and sanitary conveniences; and facilities for the storage, preparation and cooking of food and for the disposal of waste water. If a local authority is satisfied that a house is capable of being made fit at reasonable cost, a repairs notice may be served. If it is not complied with, the authority may do the work and recover the cost; appeal lies to the local county court.

If a local authority considers a house to be beyond repair at reasonable cost a repairs notice is served on the owner, the person in control of the house and mortgagees asking them to make representations. If the authority does not receive and accept an undertaking to do the repairs, it may make a demolition order, a closing order or a compulsory purchase order. A closing order is sometimes made where, although human habitation is undesirable, the property is protected as a listed building or is subject to a building preservation order. A closing order is also useful where demolition would adversely affect adjoining habitable property. A right of appeal in each case lies to the county court.

Where there are numerous unfit houses in an area a local housing authority may deal with them collectively by passing a resolution declaring the area to be a clearance area or a redevelopment area and must send a copy of its resolution to the Minister. The authority may make a clearance order requiring the owners to clear the site, purchase the land and demolish the buildings or allow redevelopment by property companies. The clearance procedure is used where the houses are unfit or by reason of their bad arrangement or the narrowness of the streets are dangerous or injurious to health and demolition is the most satisfactory solution. Redevelopment procedure can be invoked only if the area contains at least fifty houses, of which a third are overcrowded or unfit and the authority considers that the area should be redeveloped as a whole. In both cases there is detailed provision for publicity in the local press, the holding of local public inquiries in case of objection, challenge procedure in the courts and submission of the order for ministerial confirmation. Land subject to a clearance order may be purchased by agreement or compulsorily by the local authority if it is not developed within eighteen months. A redevelopment plan shows areas to be used for streets and open spaces as well as houses. Land purchased may include 'sanitary islands' of fit houses in a sea of unfit dwellings, and adjoining land. Demolition can be postponed if the houses can be made temporarily fit and are now owned by the authority, which can ask the Minister to make an order taking houses out of a clearance order. When a redevelopment plan becomes operative, the local authority can acquire land to rehouse those displaced.

In general, compensation is based on current market value in relation to fit houses which have to be acquired in a clearance or redevelopment area. In the case of condemned property in such an area, however, the basic rule is that no compensation is payable and the owner is left with the site cleared of buildings and available for development in conformity with building regulations and planning control. In the case of compulsory purchase of an unfit house, the compensation payable by the local authority is based on site value but this must not exceed the market value of the site with the useless house on it, since a cleared site available for development may be more valuable than one containing slums. The Minister may order an extra payment to be made if the house has been well maintained and an owner of a house used for business purposes will receive full compensation. Discretionary payments may be made in respect of removal expenses and losses caused by disturbance of trade or business. A 'home loss' payment may now be made to an occupier of slum property under the Land Compensation Act, 1973.

Several Housing Acts have attempted to deal with the problems of overcrowding and houses in multiple occupation, notably those of 1957, 1961 and 1964. None appear to have been very successful, perhaps because they have not been rigidly applied and enforced. The Acts prescribe penalties for offences and drastic powers are available under the 1964 Act to make a control order in respect of a house in multiple occupation if this is necessary to protect the safety, welfare or health of the occupants. There is a right of appeal to the county court and the effect of an order is to give the local authority right of possession, management and insurance. In effect the authority displaces the owner for five years and in fact the Act describes the owner as 'the dispossessed proprietor'. He must be paid compensation in lieu of rent and allowed access. The 1969 Act defines a house in multiple occupation as one occupied by persons who do not form a single household.

We now turn to the more positive and stimulating aspects of housing administration, the provision of new houses. This can be done by means of acquisition, erection of houses, conversions and improvements; and shops, recreation grounds and amenities can also be provided to service housing estates.

A local housing authority is responsible for the general management and control of its houses and flats, which it can regulate by means of by-laws and tenancy agreements. The amount of rents used to be within the discretion of the authority but they must be reasonable and subject to periodical review. Reasonableness may be a question for the courts, which expect local authorities to act as trustees for the general body of ratepayers and to balance this duty against that owed to a special class such as council tenants. Unduly low rents must not cast too heavy a load on the general rate fund; and the treasurer and auditors must be satisfied with the position of the housing revenue account. Provided that these criteria were met, a local housing authority can perfectly well operate a differential rents scheme or a rent rebate scheme based on tenants' incomes; or it might prefer to charge standard rents, leaving the poorer tenants to apply to the Department of Health and Social Security for rent relief and thus cast the burden on taxation rather than the rates. The situation has been radically altered by the Housing Finance Act, 1972, which was based on the White Paper *Fair Deal for Housing* (Cmnd. 4728, July 1971, H.M.S.O.). The concept has been borrowed from the Rent Act, 1968, under which 'fair rents' could be fixed by rent officers for private dwellings. The 1972 Act's provision means that local authorities could no longer charge differential rents for council houses. On the other hand, the Act enabled them to introduce rent rebate schemes for their own tenants and rent allowance schemes for private tenants living in furnished and unfurnished accommodation including housing association tenants.

Although the increases occasioned by fair rents involved in general annual increases of £52 per dwelling initially, their implementation caused tremendous political controversy. They also got caught up with the government's counter-inflation policy, but that is another story! Many Labour-controlled local authorities protested strongly to the Department and it was agreed that Birmingham could limit the increase to 65p a week and Newcastle to 35p. This was in response to detailed cases made out by these authorities on the basis of applying the financial criteria in the Act. Housing Commissioners were sent to Merthyr which then agreed to co-operate; and also to Bedwas and Machen in Wales. The Councillors at Clay Cross U.D.C. in Derbyshire refused to have anything to do with the Act's provisions, despite the government's power to cut subsidies and the individual liability of councillors for rent arrears. The Secretary of State has relieved them from the legal consequences of their action but their financial liability remains. Clay Cross has, of course, now disappeared as a separate authority under local government reorganization.

The Housing Rents and Subsidies Act, 1975, repealed those Parts of the 1972 Act which provided machinery for determining rents for council houses and which required local authorities to increase their rents. Such repeal, however, was expressed to be without prejudice to the duties under the earlier statute to operate rent rebate and rent allowance schemes. There is now a mandatory duty on local authorities periodically to review rents and a power to provide for a reasonable working balance in the Housing Revenue Account. The 1975 Act also gives the Secretary of State a reserve power to limit Council rents.

Local authorities must primarily allocate their housing to tenants who have been living in insanitary or overcrowded houses and to those with large families. Council tenants must not assign or sub-let without consent. In practice, much council housing has to be allocated to those dispossessed by planning and road widening schemes as well as by slum clearance.

The Director of Housing plays an important part in local housing administration and many local authorities issue tenants' handbooks.

The 1964 Act set up a Housing Corporation to promote the development of housing societies. Cost-rent societies provide housing at rents reflecting cost, without profit or subsidy; co-ownership societies enable a group to own collectively, each householder having a long lease. Local authorities may also help housing associations to provide housing by acquiring land and selling or leasing it to such associations. Authorities may sell or lease houses and may impose covenants and conditions limiting the price of resale within five years and limiting the rent payable.

Subject to certain conditions, county councils and local housing authorities can lend money for house purchase to the full value of the property. These powers extend to building, conversions, repairs and improvement of houses. Local housing authorities can also make discretionary improvement grants for conversions and improvements, subject to several conditions, and towards the provision of certain standard amenities such as a hot and cold water supply, fixed bath and water closet. The authority must be convinced that the dwelling will be satisfactory for at least fifteen years. An applicant who is refused a grant may ask the authority to state the reason. The 1964 Act enabled an authority to declare an area to be an improvement area in order to provide standard amenities.

The main purpose of the Housing Act, 1969, was to implement the proposals outlined in the White Paper *Old Houses into New Homes*. The Act incorporates the proposals for increasing the maximum amount of improvement and standard grants and for making conditions for them more flexible. The Act also enabled local authorities to pay special grants for works executed in respect of houses already having some standard amenities. Provision is made for the Minister to contribute towards the cost of improvement, standard and special grants. In order to declare a general improvement area the local authority must pass a resolution to that effect and publish an article in the local press and send a copy of the resolution report, map and statement to D. o. E. In London the G.L.C. exercises the improvement area powers, subject to L.B.C. agreement.

The Act also enables a control order relating to houses in multiple occupation to be followed by a C.P.O. It also redefines a house in multiple occupation as one occupied by persons who do not form a single household.

The Housing Act, 1974, extends the function of the Housing Corporation and enables grants to be given to housing associations. It provides for the declaration of housing action and priority neighbourhood areas which can include improvement areas, for more generous grants for works of improvement, repair and conversion in these areas; and for compulsory improvement of dwellings in such areas. Grants can now be made towards improvement of dwellings occupied by registered disabled persons. Thus clearance and redevelopment is geared to the maintenance of existing communities by pumping resources into the worst areas. Wholesale clearance is at last to be replaced by gradual renewal.

The Rent Act, 1968, consolidates the Rent Acts, including most of the Rent Act, 1965, under which controlled or regulated tenancies can have their rents reviewed, at the instance of landlord or tenant, by rent officers. Counties, county boroughs and London boroughs were registration areas whose clerks and town clerks were responsible for appointment, dismissal (with D. o. E. consent) and allocation of work of rent officers, whose terms of employment are, however, otherwise regulated by schemes made by the D. o. E.

The Rent Act provisions as to determination of fair rent are applied by the Housing Act, 1969, to controlled tenancies certified by the local authority as having all standard amenities for the exclusive use of occupants, and as being in general in good repair and fit for human habitation. Procedure is laid down as regards application for such qualification certificates, registration for rent after issue and appeal to the county court against refusal to issue. The effect of the issue of a qualification certificate is to specify a tenancy as a regulated tenancy under the Rent Act, 1968 and the procedure has been strengthened by the Housing Finance Act, 1972. Penalties for unlawful eviction and harassment were increased in 1973 and further protection given to furnished tenants by the Rent Act, 1974.

Housing finance is extremely intricate: the principle under the 1961 Act was that the general housing subsidy depended on the state of the local authority's finances. An authority charging economic or realistic rents received a higher rate of subsidy from the Ministry. Extra subsidies are given to certain large towns and cities with acute slum clearance problems *and* which have already incurred considerable expenditure on clearance projects. But special social need in urban areas now attracts grant and this can include housing.

The Housing Subsidies Act, 1967, introduced a new form of general subsidy aimed to relieve housing authorities from high rates of interest by payment of a subsidy assessed to amount to the excess over 4 per cent of the actual rate of interest paid. Extra subsidies continue to be paid for dwellings provided to meet special needs or which are unusually expensive. This Act also introduced an Option Mortgage Scheme designed to help house purchasers whose income is too low to enable them to obtain full tax-relief at the standard rate on their mortgage interest. Borrowers can elect to have *either* an Option Mortgage under which the government pays a subsidy to the lender *or* an ordinary mortgage with normal tax relief. The National House Builders Registration Council keeps a register of house-builders and requires all on the register to submit to various disciplines in the interests of purchasers. N.H.B.R.C. has power to remove builders from the register, taking into account standards of work including after-sales-service. The Housing Finance Act, 1972, entirely recast the system of housing subsidies and provided for no fewer than eight types of subsidy.The Housing Rents and Subsidies Act, 1975 has reduced them to four but there are really nine:

(1) Housing subsidy, comprising, (a) the basic element; (b) the new capital costs element; (c) the supplementary financing element; (d) the special element; (e) the high costs element;

(2) Modified rent rebate subsidy;

(3) Expanding towns subsidy.

(4) Transitional town development subsidy.

Future housing policy is outlined in a White Paper *Better Homes: the next priorities* (Cmnd. 5339, H.M.S.O., 1973). Rather late in the day, it is being suggested that wholesale clearance and redevelopment has gone too far and that gradual renewal is preferably based on improvement and repair to complement a phased programme of essential redevelopment on a relatively small scale. Grants for second homes, for more than standard amenities in owner-occupied home and purely for commercial profit, have been prohibited. The Conservative government's policy was to encourage the sale of council houses under existing legislation but this has been reversed by their successors. The 1972 Act enabled the Secretaries of State to authorize or require local authorities to impose conditions on the sale of houses covering a period longer than five years. In some cases sales at up to 30 per cent less than full market value can be allowed, subject to ministerial consent. Finally, limits on mortgage lending by local authorities to certain classes of borrowers has been lifted. These include sitting tenants, those high on waiting lists or displaced by slum clearance, and the homeless (Circular 68/73 D. o. E.). Important circulars relating to the Housing Act, 1974, are 159/74 (Welsh Office 254/74) and 160/74 (Welsh Office 266/74), Improvement of Older Housing. At the time of writing, however, local authority mortgage loans have been suspended owing to the economic crisis.

ENVIRONMENTAL HEALTH

Public health functions may be discharged by district councils, joint boards and port health authorities. The Secretary of State may by order constitute a port health authority having jurisdiction over the port and its waters and comprising one local authority or a joint board representing local authorities and the harbour authority. The modern public health authorities in part replaced the old sanitary districts; they were therefore responsible for sanitation and buildings. The local authorities must accordingly maintain and repair the public sewers and were under a general duty to provide such public sewers as may be necessary for effectual drainage. An authority can construct public sewers in streets and through private land but in both cases notice must be given and in the latter case compensation may be payable. If a private developer proposes to construct a drain or sewers and were under a general duty to provide such public sewers as system, the authority bearing the extra cost. An owner or occupier of premises has the right to drain into a public sewer. Where plans are submitted under building regulations the authority must reject them unless adequate provision is made for drainage. Subject to certain conditions, the local authority may require new buildings to be drained into a sewer. If an existing building has no satisfactory drainage system or if a drain is defective, the owner may be compelled to carry out remedial work. Environmental health officers may require stopped-up drains to be remedied within forty-eight hours of service of a notice. If a drain is believed to be defective the authority may excavate for testing purposes, reinstating and making good if it is in order. Regional Water Authorities are now responsible for sewerage (including the examination and testing of drains) and sewage disposal but district councils can discharge sewerage functions on their behalf (this is known as a 'controlled function'). District councils must provide vehicles and equipment to maintain the sewers and R.W.A.s will reimburse expenditure. R.W.A.s must not delegate responsibility for sewage disposal, trade effluent control or the financing of sewerage. If a district council and the R.W.A. agree that there should be a controlled function the R.W.A. discharges the sewerage function.

The Building Regulations, 1972, (they were first made in 1965; the 1972 Regulations have already been amended twice) regulate numerous matters previously covered by the building by-laws. The Regulations are made by the Minister and applied locally by the authorities. Plans submitted under building regulations must provide for satisfactory sanitary accommodation; and the local authority may require installation of water closets in place of other types provided that a sufficient water supply and sewer are available. The authority can require alteration or removal of new buildings which contravene the regulations or which have been erected without plans having been deposited; it also has powers to deal with dilapidated or dangerous buildings. It is important to distinguish between public health control under the building regulations and planning control of development.

Next, a local public health authority can invoke the abatement notice procedure to deal with nuisances which are 'prejudicial to health'. If service of notice does not jolt the occupier to put the matter right, the local justices can make a 'nuisance order' requiring abatement and execution of works. Appeal lies to the Crown Court and non-compliance subjects the defaulter to fines and enables the authority to do the work and recover the cost from the occupier. The courts have held that lack of internal decorative repair and noisy animals cannot be statutory nuisances. A special type of nuisance order can be sought, under the Noise Abatement Act, 1960, by the local authority or the aggrieved occupiers of land or premises.

Notices prohibiting recurrences of nuisances can now be served and justices can make a nuisance order if a prohibition notice is disregarded.

One of the most important duties of a public health authority is refuse collection: this is almost a personal service, amongst this welter of sewers, drains, sanitation and nuisances. The authority may undertake the removal of house refuse and if the council passes a resolution to do so, the duty can be enforced by an occupier of premises in the area. It can also remove trade refuse but in this case reasonable charges can be made and the duty can again be enforced. In the former case the authority may require the provision of regulation dustbins. When the Local Government Bill was passing through Parliament an amendment to allocate refuse disposal as well as refuse collection to the districts was carried in the Commons. However, the government reversed this in the House of Lords and the two functions are split between the two tiers, as in London.

Environmental health officers are also involved in consumer protection; and in smoke control enforcement under the Clean Air Acts of 1956–68. Control of infectious disease and food poisoning and enforcement of food and drug legislation has been transferred to the new R.H.A.s. However, as part of their responsibility for environmental and consumer protection, district councils can still ensure sufficiency and wholesomeness of water supplies. They can even require R.W.A.s to provide a piped water supply on certain conditions. The old sanitary inspector became the public health inspector and he now emerges as an environmental health officer. Consumer protection now looms large, particularly since the enactment of the Trade Descriptions Act, 1972. The weights and measures inspectorate of the new councils also have a part to play in this area. Authorized officers of a local authority have a right of entry at all reasonable hours under the Public Health Acts, on giving at least twenty-four hours' notice and if they are refused entry they may apply for a warrant from the justices. Finally, the occupier of land to be used as a caravan site must hold a site licence granted by the local authority, but only if planning permission has been given. This is subject to certain exceptions and conditions may be imposed which reasonably relate to the use of the land for stationing caravans. The Caravan Sites Act, 1968, restricts eviction, secures establishment of sites for use of gipsies and controls unauthorized occupation. Metropolitan counties and districts may be required to provide sites for gipsies.

IV Highways and transportation

HIGHWAYS

The Secretary of State is the highway authority for motorways and trunk roads but he can delegate his functions to local authorities, who can act as his agents to carry out repair and maintenance works. County councils are the local highway authorities for all other roads in their areas.

The Minister can direct that a road shall be a trunk road and both he and the local highway authorities can construct special roads and acquire land for construction and improvement of highways. Local authorities can acquire by agreement with the owner land near a highway if this is desirable to prevent the erection of buildings detrimental to the view from the highway or to preserve amenities. A link with the principles of planning legislation can be discerned here.

Highways repairable by a highway authority are now known as 'highways maintainable at the public expense'. Under the Highways Act, 1835, they were 'highways repairable by the inhabitants at large' and originally this had a literal meaning. As time went on the surveyors of highways came to authorize the necessary work on the authority of local highway boards, the predecessors in this respect of the local authorities, which now have a positive duty to maintain and repair such highways. Local highway authorities are now liable both for mis-feasance (negligent or unskilful repair) and non-feasance (complete lack of repair).

Where a bridge across a river carries a maintainable highway the local authority is responsible for repair of the bridge. The Minister is responsible for bridges carrying motorways or trunk roads. British Rail is responsible, as successor in title to the old railway companies, for any bridge which was built over or beneath a railway in substitution for a highway, which had been rendered unsuitable by the original works. The body responsible for repair of a bridge built before 1835 must repair the road on each side of it up to a distance of 300 feet. If the bridge was built after that date, the authority responsible for the highway before it was built remains liable for repair. Public highways and bridges must be maintained in a condition fit to accommodate ordinary traffic, in accordance with prevailing conditions. The fact that nowadays this connotes enormous lorries carrying huge loads which should travel by rail is just unfortunate. Juggernaut departments of state do not appear capable of dealing with juggernaut lorries.

A highway authority has power to make up private streets under the 'Code of 1892' The frontagers of houses in private streets can be compelled to 'make up' the street, that is to pave, sewer and light it. The local authority may apportion the cost on the basis of degree of benefit to particular premises. This is equitable; the necessary works will be more beneficial to a house at the corner of the street than to one in the middle. There are detailed rights of appeal, both to the local justices and to the Minister. The Advance Payments Code was introduced in 1951 and requires payment of the estimated cost of street works or security to be given by developers to the local authority before new buildings are erected in private streets. If more than half of the total frontage of the street is built up and the code has been applied to at least one building, a majority of the frontagers may compel the local authority to make up the street.

A highway authority may prescribe building lines and improvement lines for houses and make new street by-laws. There is authority to break up streets in various statutes and procedure is laid down in the Public Utilities Street Works Act, 1950. The theory is that breaking-up of streets for the purposes of local authorities and public corporations should be co-ordinated, so that opening up by the public health authority to look at the sewers is not followed by breaking-up by the Gas Corporation to repair a gas main and then by the Area Electricity Board to examine a cable. However, this seems to remain a pious hope, perhaps because the various bodies are not sufficiently 'down to earth'.

There is a detailed and complicated procedure for stopping up and diversion of a highway, each of which can be ordered by a magistrates' court. A highway can be stopped up as unnecessary or diverted if the proposed new road is 'nearer or more commodious to the public'. These are Highways Act powers but a local authority may also extinguish a public right of way over land purchased for slum clearance; and the Minister may authorize stopping up or diversion to enable development to be carried out in accordance with planning permission. There are the usual provisions for publicity, public inquiry in case of objection and challenge in the Courts.

A highway authority has a Common Law duty to prevent and remove obstructions; and, under the Highways Act, it can prosecute persons who cause an obstruction of the highway.

Districts, parish and community councils are responsible for footway lighting systems, whilst county councils administer road lighting (the Secretary of State in the case of trunk and special roads). Under the Highways Act, 1971, as amended, highway authorities can enter into agreements with building owners for provision of walkways and dedication of rights of way. Local authorities may prosecute persons who drop and leave litter in any public place. Local authorities have powers to number houses and to name and alter the names of streets.

Capital grants are payable to local highway authorities towards the cost of construction or improvement of principal roads. Expenditure on road maintenance is now grant aided through the rate support grant.

TRANSPORTATION

Under the Local Government Act, 1972, county councils have a duty to develop policies to promote co-ordination of public passenger transport. District councils operating transport undertakings must conform to county council policy. Both types of authority can make grants towards the cost of such operation and all public passenger transport operators, including British Rail, must co-operate with each other. A departmental Working Party reported in July 1973 on the requirements of bus operation in residential and industrial areas. Matters of local and detailed concern include location of bus stops, provision of shelters, speed, safety and punctuality of the service.

The Act gives county councils wide powers to promote the co-ordination, amalgamation and reorganization of road passenger transport undertakings. Provision is made for the various operators, including British Rail, to establish companies under the Companies Acts to hold assets.

These new powers will be important, particularly in the metropolitan counties. Four Passenger Transport Areas were designated under the Transport Act, 1968 (Greater Manchester, Merseyside, Tyneside and the West Midlands). These are now metro-counties and, with South and West Yorkshire, become P.T.A.s. This was because in the 'passenger transport areas' municipal transport undertakings were vested in passenger transport executives under the direct control of P.T.A.s. A White Paper *Urban Transport Planning* (Cmnd. 5366, H.M.S.O., 1973) proposes a system of transport supplementary grants and National Parks supplementary grants. The Local Government Act, 1974 provides that the Secretary of State shall make supplementary grants for transport purposes (commencing in the year 1975/76) to county councils and the G.L.C. in respect of estimated expenditure for:

(1) public transport;
(2) highways;

(3) the regulation of traffic;
(4) the provision of parking places.

They afford an opportunity to implement aspects of the Bains Report and to utilize the expertise available in both the public and private sectors, possibly on an advisory or part-time basis. The Department of Environment has indicated (Circular 104/73, Welsh Office 193/73) that the government intends to replace the present system of specific grants for local transport by a new unified system including current and capital expenditure on public transport and roads.

FURTHER READING

Dobry, G.: Review of the Development Control System.
Foren, R. and Brown, M.: *Planning for Service*, London (Charles Knight, 1971).
Heap, D.: *Outline of Planning Law* (Sweet and Maxwell, 1969).
Local Authority Housing Programmes – Joint Circular D.o.E. 70/74, Welsh Office 111/74.
Taylor, G., and Saunders, J. B.: *New Law of Education*, London (Butterworth, 1971).
N.A.L.G.O.: *Housing – the Way Ahead* (1973).
Housing Act, 1974: Improvement of Older Housing (D.o.E. Circular 160/74).
Housing Act, 1974: Renewal Strategies (D.o.E. Circular 13/75).
Housing Act, 1974: Housing Action Areas, Priority Neighbourhoods and General Improvement Areas. (D.o.E. Circular 14/75).
Housing Act, 1974: Needs and Action (D.o.E. Circular 24/75).

Questions

1. 'Central government departments are becoming increasingly involved in the shaping of local policy.' Discuss, with particular reference to education, social services or town and country planning.
2. Discuss the operation of the Housing Finance Act, 1972, in relation to rent rebates and rent allowances. Why was this measure so controversial politically? What is the position now?
3. Outline a policy on transportation for a metropolitan county council.
4. In the case of an outbreak of infectious disease in the area of a district council, who would perform the functions formerly discharged by the Medical Officer of Health? Give reasons for your answer and outline the action to be taken.

4 LOCAL GOVERNMENT FINANCE

Rates

DISTRICT COUNCILS are rating authorities; the Metropolitan Police Receiver, the G.L.C. county councils, joint boards and parish councils are precepting authorities. A rating authority *collects* the rates from the ratepayers in its area; a precepting authority *requires* a rating authority to collect rates payable to the former. A precept is a demand from one authority to another to collect rates. The reverse side of the rate demand shows all the services provided, the amount in the £ charged to each and the local authority responsible for each service.

The general rate, which after collection is payable into the general rate fund, is at a uniform amount in the £ on the rateable value of each hereditament (a plot or parcel of land, usually with a building on it) in the area of the local rating authority. This is known as the 'rate poundage', in other words so many pence in the pound. The number of pence can exceed 100 but this does not mean that the ratepayer is drained of every penny he possesses. For example, Henry Hopkins lives at No. 1, Acacia Avenue, Bigtown, of which he is the owner-occupier. The rateable value of this desirable property has been assessed at £200. Bigtown Borough Council declare a rate poundage of 75p in the £. This means that Henry will have to pay the rating authority £150 during the course of the financial year. The local rating authority passes a resolution in February or March declaring the rate poundage for the ensuing financial year, which for local government purposes begins on 1 April. Notice of the rate must be given within seven days after it is made by notice in public places or in the local press, and forms of demand note have been prescribed. A ratepayer has a right to be given a statement of rates payable in respect of any hereditament for which he is liable. If he wishes to challenge the legality of a rate demand note (e.g. on the ground that the authority has not followed the correct procedure in making or giving notice of the rate or that it contains an arithmetical or clerical error), the ratepayer can appeal to the Crown Court. If a ratepayer does not pay within seven days of demand, the rating authority may seek a distress warrant in the local magistrates' court. If a warrant is issued, the defaulter's goods can be seized from his home.

In practice, a rating authority will wait a good deal longer than a week before invoking this drastic procedure. A warrant of commit ment to prison may not be issued unless wilful refusal or culpable neglect is established to the satisfaction of the Court. A person aggrieved by the levy of distress upon his goods may appeal to the Crown Court.

For many years some progressive authorities have accepted payment by monthly, or even weekly, instalments. Demand notes are usually sent out half-yearly, in some areas quarterly, so that the system connotes prompt payment of fairly large sums. The Minister has encouraged local authorities to operate instalment payments and the Rating Act, 1966 requires local rating authorities to allow payments by this method on the request of ratepayers.

Until 1950 local rating authorities were responsible for assessment of rateable values as well as for the collection and spending of the rates but in that year valuation assessment functions were transferred to valuation officers of the Board of Inland Revenue. In theory, a new valuation list must be prepared quinquennially but in fact the last few were in 1939, 1956, 1963, and 1973, when rating authorities issued detailed information in bringing New Valuation Lists to the notice of the public. The valuation officer has power to require owners and occupiers of hereditaments to furnish him with returns; to obtain information from his colleague the local Inspector of Taxes as to annual values, and to inspect premises. An aggrieved ratepayer may serve a proposal to amend the list on the valuation officer, who may also make a proposal. The rating authority may make a proposal to include a hereditament if the valuation officer refuses to do so. The valuation officer must notify his proposals to the rating authority and to occupiers, who may lodge objections. Appeal from the valuation officer's decision lies to the local valuation court, a local administrative tribunal drawn from a panel of members appointed under a scheme prepared by the county council and approved by the Minister. Local valuation courts sit in public and have now been brought within the purview of the Council of Tribunals so that their constitution and working can be reviewed by that body. The valuation list can be altered following agreement by the parties or by direction of the court. Appeal lies from the local valuation court to the Lands Tribunal, which is composed of lawyers and expert valuers.

Valuation Assessment Appeal Procedure

Valuation Officer
|
Local Valuation Court
|
Lands Tribunal
|
Court of Appeal (Civil Division) (on a point of law)
|
House of Lords (with leave, on a point of law)

Rates are levied on the *occupiers* of property as a general rule; a rating authority has a permissive power to rate the owners of small properties if their rateable values do not exceed £200. Modern rating law derives from the Poor Relief Act, 1601. Over the centuries the courts of law have evolved certain tests of rateable occupation:

(1) Actual occupation
Thus empty houses are not rateable, but it has been held that seaside bungalows which remain empty in the winter but are ready for letting in the summer are rateable. Similarly, empty warehouses ready for use are in rateable occupation.

(2) Exclusive occupation.
A mere lodger is not in rateable occupation but a flat is classified as a separate hereditament and the tenant is therefore rateable. Although rates may be payable by the landlord under a lease or agreement, the demand note would be properly served by the local rating authority upon the tenant as occupier.

(3) The possession must be of some value or benefit.
Local authorities have been held rateable in respect of premises occupied for library purposes because the occupation is beneficial in the sense that public duties are being discharged. But 'land struck with sterility' is not rateable, for example, a public park, unless substantial income is derived from refreshment kiosks, amusement arcades, etc.

(4) The possession must not be temporary.
As one judge said, the occupation must be as a settler, not as a wayfarer. It has been held that a caravan occupied

as a dwelling-house is in rateable occupation. But if the use is only occasional, it would not be rateable for the occupation would then be too transient.

The Local Government Act, 1974 enables rating authorities to levy rates at up to 100 per cent on unoccupied property and to levy them selectively on different classes of unoccupied property and in different parts of an authority's area.

There is a detailed statutory formula for the calculation of the rateable value of a dwelling-house. In the first place, the *gross value* is the reasonable annual rent payable on the basis that the tenant pays usual rates and taxes and the landlord pays the cost of repairs, insurance and maintenance. In order to calculate the *rateable value*, certain deductions are made for repairs, insurance and maintenance. This is the figure entered in the valuation list by the valuation officer. What happens if the house is owner-occupied and there is no tenant paying rent? If there is no tenant, it is necessary to invent one and so the amorphous figure of the hypothetical tenant enters upon the scene. The valuation officer must seek another house as similar as possible to the owner-occupied house in every respect except one, which is that the second house *is* let. He works out his assessment on the second house and then, other things being equal, applies it to the first, which thus acquires a hypothetical tenant paying rent.

Until 1963, valuations were based on rental values obtaining in 1939 but the artificiality of this was accentuated by the operation of the Rent Act, 1957, which enabled many rents to soar to dizzy heights. The position now is that rateable values are calculated by reference to estimated current rental values. With the concept of fair rents and extension of rent control under the Rent Act, 1968, the calculation of rateable values on this basis should reach a fair middle-of-the-road level. Offices, shops, mines, factories and workshops are assessed on a slightly different basis. The rateable value of commercial and industrial hereditaments is the reasonable annual rent payable on the basis of the tenant paying all usual rents and taxes and bearing the cost of repairs, insurance and maintenance. In this case the valuation officer makes all the calculations but in the case of a dwelling-house the statutory deductions for repairs, insurance and maintenance are laid down in statutory instruments.

Until 1963 industrial hereditaments were not fully rated and a temporary concession was made in respect of shops. In 1929 industrial and freight-transport hereditaments were relieved of three-quarters of their rates; in 1958 this was reduced to a half and the partial de-rating was finally abolished in 1963, when the 20 per cent temporary concession to shopkeepers also terminated. Agricultural land and buildings were fully de-rated in 1929 and do not therefore appear at all in the valuation list. This has not been altered, despite the subsidies payable following the annual price review in the spring. The incidence of land drainage rates and charges is minimal and does not compensate for agricultural de-rating. Crown property is technically exempt from rateability owing to the doctrine of the royal prerogative: it would be inappropriate to compel the Crown to pay rates. Nevertheless, the Treasury makes a contribution in lieu of rates in respect of Crown property on the basis of valuation by the Treasury Valuer, who is of course a colleague of the valuation officer, since the Board of Inland Revenue is a department of the Treasury. For this purpose, Crown property includes police stations, owing to the law enforcement duties of the police and their historic connection with the maintenance of the Queen's Peace. In this case, the police authorities make contributions to the rating authorities in aid of the rates in much the same way as the Treasury Valuer does in respect of other Crown property. Places of public worship are also exempt and this includes church and chapel halls, unless they are let for payment which exceeds the expenses of letting.

The Rating and Valuation Act, 1961, clarified the law relating to remissions and exemptions of hereditaments occupied for charitable and ancillary purposes. There is provision for certain hereditaments to be charged no more than half the rate: these include those wholly or mainly used for charitable purposes, almshouses and houses occupied by clergymen. Moreover, the local authority has a discretion to remit or reduce further payment of rates in respect of such hereditaments and to remit or reduce rates of hereditaments occupied by certain non-profit-making organizations. The latter comprise those whose main objects are charitable, religious, educational, recreational or devoted to social welfare, science, literature and the fine arts.

There are certain other exemptions and special cases. The Secretaries of State for Education and the Environment have jointly made regulations on the valuation of county and voluntary schools based on the estimated cost of providing school places. In accordance with the principles outlined above, if a voluntary school is a charitable organization the local authority *must* give a 50 per cent remission, which it *may* increase. Other miscellaneous exemptions include public sewers, garages for certain classes of invalid carriages and land occupied for specified purposes by land drainage authorities.

Special provision has been made for the rating of hereditaments occupied by electricity, gas, transport and water undertakings. The

Boards of British Rail and British Waterways make payments in lieu of rates. Premises occupied by any of the transport boards as a dwelling house, hotel or place of public refreshment are fully rated. There is a statutory formula for the payment of rates by the Central Electricity Generating Board and the Area Electricity Boards; but premises used as a dwelling-house or showrooms and premises occupied by the Electricity Council are rated in the ordinary way. Again, the Gas Corporation is rateable under a statutory formula under the Gas Act, 1972. Premises occupied for operational purposes by the Gas Corporation are not liable to be rated but gas showrooms are rated in the ordinary way. Water undertakings have been assessed since 1963 under a complicated formula in the Rating and Valuation Act, 1961 and this will presumably be applied to the new R.W.A.s. The telecommunications apparatus of the Post Office is rateable under the Post Office Act, 1969. Rating and valuation law is now contained in the consolidating General Rate Act, 1967.

Grants and loans

Grants in aid of services administered locally were made by the central government in the mid-nineteenth century. At that time the government began to make 'percentage grants' to specific authorities so that they could depend upon receiving a specific proportion of the cost from monies voted by Parliament, the remainder being raised by rate. One of the first of these percentage grants was the police grant, which was introduced in 1856. The Local Government Act, 1888, however, abolished most of the old percentage grants and replaced them with 'assigned revenues'. Under this system the proceeds of taxes of a local character were assigned to the use of local authorities. This had the curious effect that the cost of education was for a time subsidized by the duty on whisky and other spirits. Changes in the national taxation and fiscal policy rendered the system of assigned revenues somewhat cumbersome and unrealistic so that it was finally abolished by the Local Government Act, 1929.

Meanwhile percentage grants had become payable for a number of services including not only the police but also education, highways, housing and some health services. Under the scheme of the 1929 Act, new 'block grants' were paid in lump sums to local authorities in respect of all the remaining services, but shortly after the end of the last war percentage grants were payable in respect of town and county planning and local health and welfare services. This, then, was the system in operation until the enactment of the Local Government

Act, 1958. Under that Act, a 'general grant' or block grant became payable for most of the main services, including education, health, welfare, planning and fire protection. Specific grants remained payable in respect of police, civil defence, housing, planning and roads.

The general grant was payable to all county councils and county borough councils and the total amount available for distribution was prescribed in a General Grant Order made by the Minister of Housing and Local Government every two years in December. The amount was calculated by reference to estimates submitted by the local authorities and the Minister had to take into account the current level of prices, costs, remuneration and expenditure; any probable fluctuation in demand for the services and the need for their development. The Order had to be approved by the Commons and the Minister had power to vary the amount during the two years. If the Minister was satisfied that a local authority had failed to achieve or maintain reasonable standards he could submit a report to Parliament and, if the report was approved by the Commons, he could reduce the amount of general grant payable. The yardstick here was the average standard achieved by other authorities in the area, taking into account also those postulated by the relevant government departments. Similarly, a specific grant was not payable unless the appropriate Minister was broadly satisfied with the service provided. Thus the power to withhold a substantial unit grant for housing tended to ensure that local rehousing schemes conform to standards prescribed by the Minister. There is no appeal against a Minister's decision to withhold a grant.

The 1929 Act provided for the payment of general exchequer grants to county councils and county borough councils, based on a complicated 'weighting' formula taking into account such matters as rateable value, children under five, the unemployed and, in the counties, population per mile of road. This system was replaced in 1948 by 'exchequer equalization grants' payable to the poorer authorities, i.e. those falling below a defined minimum standard of financial resources. Again, a 'weighted population' formula was used, similar to that of 1929. The 1948 Act also enabled county councils to pay capitation grants to their county district councils.

The financial aspects of the 1958 Act were an attempt to strengthen local government by slackening the financial control of the central government departments. It is doubtful whether this worthy aim has been achieved, since the total grant contribution of the government still considerably exceeds the income of local authorities from rates. The exchequer equalization grants were replaced by 'rate deficiency grants' and the capitation grants were abolished. Rate deficiency grants were payable to the councils of county boroughs, counties and county districts if their actual product of a rate of a penny in the £ was less than the national standard penny rate product. The formula was modified in the counties if the population was less than seventy per mile of road.

The Minister could reduce a rate deficiency grant if a reasonable standard was not being maintained by a local authority, subject to approval of his report by the House of Commons. These drastic default powers have never been invoked in relation to either the rate deficiency grant or the general grant. This is not only evidence of the general good behaviour of local authorities but also of the fact that withdrawal of necessary finance would be hardly likely to promote efficiency.

Local government finance was entirely recast by the Local Government Act, 1966, which provides for the payment of rate support grants to local authorities and abolished the general and rate deficiency grants. After consultation with the local authority associations, the Secretary of State determines the total central government grant, excluding housing subsidies. He continues to take into account the factors postulated in the 1958 Act (level of prices, costs, etc.). Grants to local authorities for rate rebates under the Rating Act, 1966, and specific grants are deducted from this total and the balance remaining constitutes the rate support grant.

The total is made up of a resources element, a needs element and a domestic element. The resources element (payable to all local authorities except parish councils) replaces the rate deficiency grant and is payable to any local authority with rate resources lower than the national average. The needs element is in substitution for the general grant and is based on population and other objective factors corresponding to the 'weighting' formulae used in older legislation. The domestic element enables a deduction to be made in rate poundages on residential property (which must be passed on to the domestic ratepayer in reduced rates).

The Act abolishes the specific grants for school milk and meals and provides for specific grants for development and redevelopment; public open space; reclamation of derelict land; port and airport health; and special expenditure due to the presence in an area of substantial numbers of immigrants from the Commonwealth whose language or customs differ from those of the community.

When the Minister has completed his calculations, he makes a rate support grant order, operative for not less than two years. The order must be laid before the House of Commons together with a report, for approval. There is provision for the making of supplementary grants (subject to the same procedure) owing to inflationary pressure. The Act enables any Minister concerned with a local service to reduce any of the elements paid to a local authority if it has fallen below an average standard, subject to allowing it to make representations and to the safeguard of laying a report before Parliament. It can thus be seen that the 1966 Act continues some well-entrenched notions: consultations; criteria to consider in formulating estimates; special aid to poorer authorities; grants for special need; and default powers. Arising from the 1973 revaluation and after representations from the local authority associations, partial relief from rate increases was made available, the government meeting a proportion of the cost.

A Green Paper, *Future Shape of Local Government Finance* (Cmnd. 4741, H.M.S.O., July 1971), foreshadowed a Local Government Bill dealing with finance but this did not appear until over two years later. The Local Government Act, 1974 merely builds on the pre-existing law. The rate support grant system with its three elements will continue as before, except that the order will be made annually and will settle how much shall be deducted to allow for specific and supplementary grants. Grants at the rate of 90 per cent will be paid in respect of the new rate rebate scheme and a new specific grant of mandatory awards and grants to students. The statutory rate rebate scheme will be calculated by reference to the needs and resources of residential occupiers. In addition, a local rating authority may make a local rate rebate scheme on similar lines. These schemes replace those under the General Rate Act, 1967, but they are alternatives, not cumulative.

It is often necessary for the cost of expensive works to be financed by loans charged on the revenues (including rates) or land of a local authority. In this way the capital cost is spread over a period of years, and loans will be sanctioned only if the works are of a permanent nature and will continue to benefit the local ratepayers.

A general borrowing power was contained in the Local Government Act, 1933. Provided that statutory authority exists for the purpose of the loan, a local authority could borrow money to acquire land or buildings, to erect buildings, to undertake permanent works or to meet any other expense which the Secretary of State for the Environment considered should be spread over a number of years. Similar powers are contained in the Local Government Act, 1972, the only restraints now being that there must be statutory authority for the expenditure and the Minister must sanction it. This Minister is the sanctioning authority, even for such services as education, and he will consider the legality of the project and the financial resources of the local authority.

The normal maximum period for the repayment of a loan is sixty years and, once sanctioned, it is charged upon all the revenues of the borrowing authority. Since 1958 local authorities have been able to operate consolidated loans funds, with the Minister's consent. This is a device for the pooling of all money borrowed.

Borrowing powers may be obtained by a local Act of Parliament for purposes for which no general power exists, but strict proof of estimates is required by Parliamentary Standing Orders and returns of expenditure must be made to the Minister. Local authorities may borrow from the open market or from the Public Works Loans Board. Local authorities can also borrow from their reserve or superannuation funds if the money is not currently required for those purposes. Local authorities have powers of investment through L.A.M.I.T. (Local Authorities Mutual Investment Trust). The scope of such powers made collectively through L.A.M.I.T. has been extended by the Local Authorities Mutual Investment Trust Act, 1968.

Audit

Under the system of district audit, the local authority must prepare a financial statement, and for seven clear days before the audit a copy of every account and all relevant vouchers and receipts must be available for inspection at the council offices by 'any person interested'. Notice of these facilities must be given by advertisement in the local press. An 'interested person' can make copies or extracts or depute an agent to do this; he is entitled to have a skilled person at his elbow, such as an accountant. 'Persons interested' include electors, ratepayers, contractors, landowners, shopkeepers and officials of trades unions whose members are employees of the local authority.

A local government *elector* may be present or may be represented at the audit and may object to any of the accounts. The qualification for the right to object to the accounts is thus more restricted than that for the right to inspect. The district auditor is a Civil Servant, being an official of the department. His powers are very wide and he can require the production of documents and can interrogate the officers responsible for them. It was the duty of the district auditor to disallow every item of the account which was contrary to law and to surcharge the amount of any expenditure disallowed upon the person responsible, be he an elected member or an appointed officer. At the conclusion of the audit he certifies his allowance of the accounts, subject to any disallowance or surcharge. An item will be 'contrary to law' if it is illegal in the sense that there is no statutory authority for the expenditure, which is accordingly *ultra vires*. Expenditure has been held to be contrary to law if it was unreasonable in extent, even though the objects were lawful. This is illustrated by the decision of the House of Lords in 1925 in the *Poplar Wage Case* (*Roberts v. Hopwood* (1925) A.C. 578), a decision which inhibited reasonable freedom of action in local government for many years.

The council of the Metropolitan Borough of Poplar (now incorporated in the London Borough of Tower Hamlets), was authorized to pay its employees reasonable wages and resolved to pay its manual workers wages in excess of those paid to similar workers by other local employers. The actual wage involved was £4 a week, but it should be borne in mind that this was fifty years ago. The district auditor disallowed most of the excess over the ordinary prevailing rates of pay as unreasonable and therefore contrary to law. He was upheld in the High Court, reversed in the Court of Appeal and finally vindicated in the House of Lords on the ground that the expenditure was excessive and therefore unlawful. The council was held not to have acted as a proper trustee of the ratepayers' money. The surcharged councillors, whose leader was George Lansbury, later leader of the Labour Party, refused to pay but the surcharge was later remitted by Neville Chamberlain, the Minister of Health (then in charge of local government).

Twenty years later, a rather more liberal decision of the Court of Appeal (*re Walker's Decision* (1944) 1 All E.R. 614) allowed the payment of children's allowances by a local authority to its employees; the total amount having been held to be reasonable. But in the *St Pancras Rents Case* (*Taylor v. Munrow* (1960) 1 All E.R. 455) the shadow of Poplar returned, the Court holding itself to be bound by the older decision of the House of Lords. In that case, the council of the Metropolitan Borough of St Pancras (now incorporated in the London Borough of Camden), was responsible for requisitioned properties and had a statutory duty to review the rents of the tenants from time to time. Owing to its dislike of the policy of the Rent Act, 1957, the council decided not to increase the rents of these tenants but to pay the balance of the increased rent to the landlords. The councillors concerned were surcharged by the district auditor and at the hearing of the appeal the Lord Chief Justice said that the council had in effect made a gift of the increase to the landlords. The case had several interesting features, one being that the councillors concerned disregarded the advice of their town clerk, always an unwise thing to do. In the *St Pancras Case* the district auditor's surcharge was upheld but the case had an even more unfortunate sequel. Appeal lay to the High Court but if the surcharge was in respect of a sum not over £500, there was a choice between appealing to the Minister or to the High Court. Some councillors appealed to the Minister, who in the circumstances relieved them from the surcharge; others appealed to the High Court, which upheld the surcharge. The net result was that quite fortuitously, fewer people had to pay the same total sum of money. That procedure was invoked in respect of a sum of £200. On a second surcharge of £1,400 the appeals had to go to the High Court and on this occasion both groups of councillors sought a declaration to avoid disqualification from council membership and applied for relief from personal liability. The court awarded the declaration but refused relief from personal liability. In general, the Minister's decision on appeal was final; and a person may apply for a declaration by the High Court or by the Minister that he acted reasonably or believed that his action was authorized by law. The Court or the Minister could relieve a councillor from payment of surcharge in whole or in part if satisfied that he 'ought fairly to be excused'. If the surcharge was in a sum exceeding £500, relief could be sought from disqualification from membership of a local authority for a period of five years; and such relief was obtained by the surcharged councillors in the *St Pancras Case*, as noted above.

No expense paid by a local authority may be disallowed by the district auditor if it has been sanctioned by the Minister. Nevertheless, if the relevant payment is *ultra vires*, a local government elector can seek an injunction or declaration in the High Court and, if he is successful, this should have the effect of preventing a recurrence of the illegal expenditure. There is provision for the Minister to direct the district auditor to hold an extraordinary audit of accounts on giving three days' written notice to the local authority. After completion of the audit the local authority must make an abstract of accounts and give notice in the local press, that it can be inspected. Local authorities contribute to the cost of district audit by a stamp duty based on the volume of transactions within the audited accounts.

The Local Government Act, 1972, has altered the audit law. The district auditor no longer has the power to surcharge and a right of appeal now lies only to the Courts. The *St Pancras Rents Case* has thus had an impact on subsequent legislation. The district auditor may certify that a loss or deficiency is due from a named person from whom the local authority may recover but that person may demand reasons in writing and appeal to the Courts. The district auditor may also apply to the High Court for a declaration that a payment is illegal; but he cannot question expenditure sanctioned by the Secretary of State. If the Court holds that the expenditure is contrary to law the offender is surcharged with the amount and if this exceeds £2,000 and he is a councillor he can be disqualified from membership for a period in the Court's discretion.

The Act requires all local authorities to elect between a system of district audit or approved audit and this had to be done before the end of 1973. The choice for parishes was made by district councils and the effect is that some accounts are subject to district audit and some to approved audit. There are provisions enabling subsequent changes to be made. Approved auditors are professionally qualified and approved by the Secretary of State to whom they can report, but local government electors have no right to appear before them and object, as in the case of district audit. The Department of the Environment has issued guidance on the approval of auditors (Circular 94/73, Welsh Office Circular 176/73). At the time of writing the Housing Finance (Special Provisions) Bill is before Parliament.

Reform

The system of local government finance has long been criticized but it is so entrenched that many attempts at reform have foundered. Rates in particular have been attacked as regressive in contradistinction to taxation, which is said to be progressive because it takes into account social factors such as earning power and family responsibilities. Although the method of valuation for rating purposes of dwelling-houses may be fair, the occupiers and ratepayers of two identical properties may be in very different circumstances: one may be wealthy, the other may be a pensioner. The remedy postulated by the Liberal Party is the rating of site values: under this system, buildings on the land would be ignored for rating valuation purposes. On the other hand, the value of the site could be enhanced considerably by the grant of planning permission for a profitable purpose and site value rating would take account of this. Even under existing procedures, the actual cost of land has been taken as the best evidence of the value of a school site.

Another suggestion, made by a study group of the Royal Institute of Public Administration in 1956, is that there should be a form of local income tax to be collected and spent by local authorities. Ever since the war all employers, including local authorities, have collected tax from their employees on behalf of the Inland Revenue under the P.A.Y.E. system. It was thought that this system could be extended to the collection of a small local tax. This would be collected by all employers in the area of a local authority and the total amount deducted from employees' salaries and wages would be passed to the local authority. The objection to this idea was that people would be taxed in respect of their work places rather than their homes, and that some local authorities, with numerous offices, factories and workshops in their areas, would benefit much more than others in the rural and more sparsely populated districts. The laudable object was to try and give local government a source of revenue independent of rates and grants but the idea foundered on the objections and was not implemented.

Under the rating law, based as it is on the concept of actual and beneficial occupation of land and buildings, unoccupied or empty property was not rateable until recently. A local Act of Parliament enabled the City of London Corporation to collect a proportion of the rates on such properties but this was the only exception. We have already noticed that seaside bungalows and warehouses are borderline cases, the acid test being whether they are ready for occupation or storage, even though they were empty during part of the rating year. There is a strong case for the rating of empty property envisaged in the Local Government Act, 1966, especially in view of the numerous large office blocks which remain unoccupied for months or even years in some of our cities. If the rating system is retained, it may well be that there should be a shift of emphasis from occupation to ownership as the test of rateability. Moreover, the rating of empty or vacant hereditaments would encourage owners to utilize their properties to the fullest possible extent. A welcome development is the provision in the Local Government Act, 1974 for 100 per cent rating of empty property, although the provision is not mandatory.

The Rating Act, 1966, enables local rating authorities to allow rebates to domestic ratepayers with low incomes. Ratepayers who qualify for a full rebate are entitled to a remission of two-thirds of the amount by which their rates exceed £7.50 a year. A childless married couple earning £14 a week qualify for full remission; an increased wage being permissible in the case of a married couple with dependent children, at the rate of £4 for each child. The Act provides an example of a useful minor reform, especially as it is coupled with the right of domestic ratepayers to elect to pay their rates by instalments. Those who can apply for rate rebates include owner-occupiers and tenants of private and council property. Again, the Local Government Act, 1974 has taken the matter further.

We have already seen that the history of grants-in-aid or government grants has been somewhat chequered. At the present time, the government meets approximately 60 per cent of local government expenditure by means of grant. Education is by far the most costly of the services provided by local authorities and some students of politics and public administration have advocated transferring its total cost to the Exchequer. This has been resisted by the spokesmen of local government on the grounds that such a development would weaken local control still further. The police services constitute another candidate for greater contributions from the central government, which currently makes a specific grant of 50 per cent of the net expenditure. Although subject to a measure of local control, the police are not really a local government service and the police grant could well be increased materially without detriment to the local authorities. Again, should the government shoulder a greater share of the burden of expenditure on the roads? The Secretary of State for the Environment is already responsible for trunk roads and motorways and important aspects of national policy are often linked with road widening and other schemes in relation to the lesser roads. The compromise solution which is expected to be implemented in the case of education could well be extended also to highways, so that the Ministry grants to local authorities could be increased. Specific grants for highways, transport and the countryside are to be terminated or modified, being replaced by supplementary grants.

There is no doubt that the payment of rates is much more unpopular than payment of taxes, partly owing to the method of collection and partly due to a feeling of injustice in some cases. Palliatives such as payment by instalments do not appear to be enough. The solution may well be for the Exchequer to assume greater responsibility for expenditure on the more important and expensive services, further candidates for special treatment being education and the police. A significant proportion of the expenditure, however, should still be met locally. The Layfield Committee has been considering proposals for reform for several months.

In the summer of 1975 a Consultative Council on local government finance was set up comprising Ministers from the spending departments (D.o.E., D.H.S.S., D.E.S., Home Office and Welsh Office and, to a lesser extent, the Departments of Employment and Industry) and leaders of the local authority associations.

FURTHER READING

H. Aughton: *Local Government Finance for District Councillors*, Chichester (Barry Rose, 1972).

Bean, P. R. and Lockwood, A.: *Rating Valuation Practice* (Stevens, 1969).

Foulkes: *The Local Government Act, 1974* (Butterworth, 1974).

Questions

1. What criticisms can be levelled against the rating system? Do you consider that a more acceptable form of local taxation could be used as an alternative or as a supplement to the rates?
2. 'A reasonable measure of financial independence is an essential element in local democracy.' Discuss.
3. What are the advantages and disadvantages of the present heavy reliance on general grants in local government finance?
4. Advise Bloggs on the action he can take if he considers that his rateable value is too high.
5. In what ways has the Local Government Act, 1972, affected the system of auditing in local government? Has case-law influenced the relevant statutory provisions?

5 POWERS OF LOCAL AUTHORITIES

By-laws

A by-law is a special form of delegated legislation made by district councils under procedure laid down in the Local Government Act, 1972 for the good rule and government of their areas and for the suppression of nuisances. After being made under the seal of the council, a by-law must be submitted to the confirming authority, who is in general the Secretary of State.

The council must publish in the local press notice of its intention to make the by-law, after which objectors have a month in which to object to the confirming authority. At the end of this period the by-law is submitted for confirmation. In deciding whether or not to confirm a by-law, the Minister will consider whether it is in fact necessary, having regard to local conditions and national policy. He must, of course, also be satisfied that the proposed by-law is *intra vires* and that it is not likely to be set aside by the Courts on other grounds. Confirming authorities have issued sets of model by-laws based on experience: this helps the local authorities to avoid pitfalls and encourages uniformity in the country as a whole. A by-law may be confirmed or rejected – a confirming order fixes its date of operation in the area of the local authority. After confirmation a copy of the by-law must be available for public inspection and sale. Numerous statutes authorize the making of by-laws (e.g. the Public Health Acts) and an enabling Act will fix the penalty for non-compliance.

In the early years, the courts laid down four judicial tests of the validity of by-laws. In the first place, a by-law must be reasonable. Thus in 1898 the House of Lords held that a by-law made by Kent County Council prohibiting any person from playing music or singing in any place within fifty yards of a dwelling-house after being requested to desist was reasonable. It was said in this case that there is a presumption of reasonableness in favour of by-laws made by local authorities because they are bodies of a public representative character entrusted by Parliament with delegated authority. Their by-laws should be supported if possible, since local authorities are elective, not nominated, bodies. The onus of proof in the courts is therefore on the person alleging that a by-law is unreasonable. A by-law will be declared void as unreasonable, however, if it discriminates unfairly between different classes of people, if it is manifestly unjust, if it discloses bad faith or if it is oppressive. The second judicial test is that a by-law should be certain in its terms and clear in its meaning. On this principle, a by-law providing that 'no person shall wilfully annoy passengers in the streets' has been held too vague and uncertain and was therefore set aside as void.

A third and most important principle is that a by-law must not conflict with the positive provisions of common law or statute. The function of a by-law is to supplement the law, not to override it; it must therefore be consistent with the general law. This is in accordance with the doctrine of the sovereignty of Parliament, for by-laws constitute a type of subordinate legislation. Only Parliament can change the general law. The fourth and last of the judicial tests is that a by-law must be *intra vires* its enabling legislation. This is a fundamental principle, not unconnected with the third test. There have not been many actions in the courts on the validity of by-laws in recent years, partly because the judicial tests are so well known and partly because the system of issuing model by-laws by the central departments has helped local authorities to avoid errors. Finally, it should be noticed that other Ministers may confirm by-laws if named as confirming authorities in the enabling enactments. For example, the Secretary of State for Education and Science is the confirming authority for by-laws made under the Public Libraries and Museums Act, 1964, and the Minister of Agriculture, Fisheries and Food confirms those made under the Food and Drugs Acts.

Acquisition of powers

If a local authority wishes to acquire new powers which are not covered by existing legislation, it must seek to promote a local or private Bill in Parliament. Thirty clear days' notice of a council meeting convened to promote a local Bill must be given in the local press and the resolution to promote it must be carried by a majority vote (ten days suffice in the case of a resolution to oppose a private Bill). The resolution is then published in the local newspapers and submitted for approval to the Secretary of State. When the local Bill has been finally deposited in Parliament, another confirmatory resolution must be passed at least fourteen days after deposit. If a council wishes to oppose a local Bill promoted by another authority, the same procedure must be followed in relation to resolutions and publicity. It should be realized that private Bills can also be introduced in Parliament on behalf of public corporations and there may well be a conflict of interest between local government and a nationalized industry, as well as between differing types of local authority.

Local authorities often used to obtain new powers by means of the provisional order procedure. Numerous Acts of Parliament gave Ministers power to make provisional orders, in the old days 'for the execution of useful works'. The local authority had to apply to the Minister for an order, after having given interested parties an opportunity to object by means of a notice in the *London Gazette* and the local press. If objections were raised, a local inquiry was normally held and the Minister then made a provisional order. The order had no force until included in a Provisional Orders Confirmation Bill, a special kind of local Bill subject in other respects to the usual parliamentary procedure for a local Bill. If a petition was presented before confirmation the petitioner could appear before the Select Committee in both Houses and oppose the order. An advantage of the procedure was that it enlisted a measure of government support in Parliament but it came to be regarded as rather cumbersome, having to pass through all stages of a local Bill in both Houses.

The Statutory Orders (Special Procedure) Acts, 1945–65, enable an order to be made by a Minister, who lays it before Parliament after compliance with preliminary proceedings in the enabling Act. If no procedure is specified, notice must be given in the *London Gazette* and in the local press. The notice must state the procedure for lodging objections and the Minister has a discretionary power to hold a local inquiry. Petitions may be lodged within twenty-one days of laying before Parliament. All petitions are referred to the Chairman of Ways and Means and the Lord Chairman of Committees who report to each House if objections have been made and if they can be received. Petitions for amendment pray for special amendments and are referred to a joint committee of both Houses; petitions of general objection pray against the order generally but are referred to a joint committee only if either House of Parliament so resolves.

The Joint Committee consists of three members of both Houses and it can report the order with or without amendment; in the latter case, it comes into operation on the day the report is laid before Parliament. If the order is amended it will take effect on a day fixed by the Minister. If the Minister has second thoughts arising from the petitions and objections, he may withdraw the order or resubmit it to Parliament by means of a Provisional Order Confirmation Bill. Many statutes passed since 1945 provide for orders made under them to be subject to special parliamentary procedure and it has been extended to earlier legislation by Order-in-Council. The advantage of this post-war procedure to Parliament and to local government is that it is much quicker. Special parliamentary procedure was applied to the power to repeal, alter or amend local Acts for public health purposes (under the Public Health Act, 1875), but in 1962 provisional order procedure was restored in order to ensure greater parliamentary scrutiny in these matters.

Acquisition of land

There are a great number of statutes affecting the power of local authorities to acquire land; these include the Local Government Act, 1972; the Public Health Acts, 1875–1961; the Acquisition of Land (Authorisation Procedure) Act, 1946; the Land Compensation Acts, 1961–73; the Town and Country Planning Act, 1972; and the Compulsory Purchase Act, 1965. All local authorities have a general power to acquire land by agreement by means of purchase, lease or exchange of land. This covers the acquisition of land in advance of requirements and in this case Ministerial consent is necessary, as it is for loan sanction in connection with acquisition by agreement. Parish and community councils can acquire by agreement under a Public General Act.

County and district councils can acquire land compulsorily for the purpose of any of their functions under a public or private Act of Parliament. We have already seen that development plans may allocate land for the purpose of *any* of the functions of a local authority; education, social services, housing, highways, planning or transportation, for example. If the land is expressly designated as subject to compulsory purchase, a local authority may be authorized to acquire the land compulsorily.

The first step is for the local authority to make a compulsory purchase order (C.P.O.) describing the land and to publish a notice in the local press, indicating where the order and map may be inspected and how objections may be made. A similar notice must be served on owners, occupiers and lessees of the land. The draft order is then sent to the relevant Minister who must hold a local inquiry or private hearing if there are objections. If the Minister confirms the order the authority must give public notice of confirmation in the local press and this publication is the date upon which the order comes into effect. A C.P.O. can be challenged within six weeks of this date by a special appeal to the High Court to quash it on the grounds that it is *ultra vires* or that the interests of the appellant have been substantially prejudiced by failure to comply with a statutory requirement. An aggrieved person must invoke this challenge procedure quickly, for if proceedings are not started within six weeks, the order may not be questioned in any legal proceedings whatsoever, even if fraud or bad faith are alleged: *Smith v. East*

Elloe R.D.C. (1956) 1 All E.R. 855. However an acquiring authority must exercise its powers within three years from date of operation of C.P.O.

Special parliamentary procedure must be followed if objection is made to a C.P.O. affecting land belonging to a local authority or held inalienably by the National Trust. This procedure also applies if the C.P.O. relates to the site of an ancient monument unless the Secretary of State has certified that the acquiring authority has undertaken to safeguard the monument. Similarly, special parliamentary procedure applies if the C.P.O. relates to commons, allotments or open spaces, unless the relevant Minister certifies that the land is required for road widening or that it will be replaced by equally suitable land; and to operational land of statutory undertakers (e.g. C.E.G.B., N.C.B., Gas Corporation).

A district council can acquire land for a parish council after holding a local inquiry. The resultant C.P.O. is subject to Ministerial confirmation or modification in the ordinary way. The district council then acquires the land and conveys it to the parish council, which has the right to appeal to the Minister if the council refuses to make an order.

When a C.P.O. has become operative, the acquiring authority may serve on the owner a Notice to Treat and this has the same effect as if the owner had entered into a contract to sell to that authority. The Lands Tribunal is available to settle disputes on compensation payable if the parties cannot agree. The acquiring authority may at any time after service of Notice to Treat give Notice of Entry on the land, to take effect not less than fourteen days after service. If Notice to Treat is not served within three years of the coming into force of the C.P.O., the order lapses.

We have seen in Chapter 3 that compensation for compulsory purchase is in general based on the current market value. However there was considerable public disquiet about loss of amenities, disturbance and what is known generically as 'injurious affection', particularly with regard to motorway and other road developments. A White Paper *Development and Compensation: putting people first* (Cmnd. 5124) was presented to Parliament in October 1972, and the Land Compensation Act, 1973, improves the position considerably. D. O. E. Circular 73/73 (Welsh Office 132/73) indicated that two matters required immediate attention – home loss payments and advance payments of 90 per cent of compensation where possession has been taken of a claimant's land, subject to satisfactory evidence of title. The Act gives a right to compensation for injurious affection to owners of houses; and owner-occupiers of residential property, farms and other premises with rateable value up to £2,250 (the limit does not apply to an owner's interest alone). Depreciation must arise from physical factors caused by use of highways, aerodromes and other public works such as dust, fumes, noise, vibration. Interest on compensation from date of claim, legal and valuation fees are also payable. The injurious effect of public works is also mitigated by power to make sound insulation regulations and to pay expenses of removals caused by nuisance of construction works.

Highway authorities can now acquire owner-occupied land severely affected by construction and road works. Special home loss payments can be made to people displaced from their homes by compulsory purchase, redevelopment or clearance under the Housing Acts. This is not dependent on any right to compensation or disturbance payment but it is a discretionary payment and cannot be paid under the blight notice procedure. There can also be similar farm loss and disturbance payments and, most important, a mandatory rehousing provision related to compulsory acquisition or redevelopment and demolition, closing or clearance under the Housing Acts. The Act also improves the law on compensation for injurious affection by relating assessment to the whole of the works and also makes better provision for compensation for outright acquisition where those concerned are disabled, small businessmen over sixty or farmers. Finally, the Act considerably extends the power under the Town and Country Planning Act, 1971, to serve blight notices where land has depreciated in value owing to development proposals. This can now be done in relation to proposals and modifications in structure and local plans; highway orders or schemes; C.P.O.s; new town orders; slum clearance and new street orders. Parliament did well in enacting this statute, which was long overdue. The Land Community Bill is now before Parliament: if it is enacted and not repealed, it will be described in a subsequent edition.

Relations between authorities

We now turn to a description of the local government associations, which have an honourable and important part to play in representing the various classes of local authority.

THE LOCAL AUTHORITY ASSOCIATIONS UP TO 1974

The local authority associations are recognized by government departments as representative national bodies and are consulted on legislation and subordinate legislation, circulars and policy matters. Government departments often seek the views of the associations informally on the practical application of proposals. Departmental committees often invite the associations to submit memoranda of evidence and government departments frequently assemble small working parties to examine special problems such as model standing orders or rate support grants. The associations may be asked to nominate representatives to serve on working parties.

THE ASSOCIATION OF MUNICIPAL CORPORATIONS (1873–1974)

This was the oldest of the local authority associations, having been founded at a time when all municipal boroughs enjoyed the same status. With the creation of county boroughs in 1888, the membership embraced both types of municipal corporation. The metropolitan borough councils became eligible for membership as did their successors the London borough councils. There were nearly 400 member corporations.

THE COUNTY COUNCILS ASSOCIATION (1889–1974)

The Association consisted of fifty-eight county councils in England and Wales and its objects were to watch over and protect the interests, rights and privileges of county councils, as representatives of the county electorate, as they might be affected by legislation of general application to counties. The Association was represented on some thirty negotiating bodies, and there was a separate Association of County Councils in Scotland.

THE URBAN DISTRICT COUNCILS ASSOCIATION (1895–1974)

This Association was the direct lineal successor of the Association of Local Boards of Health, which were the predecessors of the original urban district councils that came into existence in 1895. In effect, the Association merely changed its name. 100 per cent membership was achieved some thirty years ago. This was maintained, so that all the 522 urban district councils in England and Wales were members of the Association.

THE RURAL DISTRICT COUNCILS ASSOCIATION (1895–1974)

The Association was formed in 1895 following the creation of rural district councils as successors to the rural sanitary authorities. There were 469 rural district councils in membership of the Association, full membership having been achieved in 1953. The objects of the Association were to protect the rights and interests of the rural district councils as they might be affected by legislation; and to assist in maintaining a high standard of administration of the public services in rural districts.

The local authority associations in 1974

THE ASSOCIATION OF COUNTY COUNCILS

The first meeting of this Association was held in October 1973. All fifty-three county councils in England and Wales and the G.L.C. are eligible for membership. The framework of a Constitution has been approved in principle. Member councils appoint representatives on the basis of their population and each will be entitled to vote. Dissenting views of particular types of member councils may be recorded and submitted to government departments. The Committee structure includes a standing committee of metropolitan county councils. On matters exclusive to Wales, the Welsh Counties will deal directly with the government through a Welsh Counties Committee. It is the declared objective of the new Association to aim at the establishment of a single organization to speak for and represent local government in England and Wales. The Association is the direct successor of the County Councils Association.

THE ASSOCIATION OF METROPOLITAN AUTHORITIES

This new Association was formed on 31 July 1973, and comprises six metropolitan counties, thirty-six metropolitan district councils, thirty-two London borough councils, the Greater London Council, the Inner London Education Authority and the City of London Corporation. Its objects are to promote the interests of its members particularly in relation to legislation; to provide a forum for discussion, especially having regard to negotiations with government departments; and to provide common services. Each authority in membership is entitled to one vote at meetings of the Association, which has a Policy Committee and functional committees dealing with the major local government services. The Association meets at least four times a year. At the time of writing, the A.M.A. is opposed to a single association and even, apparently, to a federation of associations.

THE ASSOCIATION OF DISTRICT COUNCILS

This new Association was formed in November 1973 and represents 333 shire district councils in England and Wales. Its objects are similar to those of the A.M.A. and include joining with the other associations to promote the interests of local government and to provide central services. There is a Policy Committee and a Committee for Wales. It should be noted that the member-authorities of this Association are drawn from local authorities formed from the amalgamation of pre-existing borough, urban and rural district councils. The Association therefore has many members with experience of service in the A.M.C., R.D.C.A. and U.D.C.A. In view of the attitude of A.M.A. A.D.C. has decided not to pursue the possibility of a federation of new associations for the time being.

FEDERATION OF ASSOCIATIONS

Of the former associations, C.C.A. and U.D.C.A. were in favour of a single association but the others were not. Of the new, A.C.C. has declared in favour of the principle but the attitude of A.M.A. and A.D.C. is uncertain. However, the four former associations (C.C.A., A.M.C., R.D.C.A., U.D.C.A.) together with the London Boroughs Association, agreed in principle that there should be a single strong central federation of local authority associations of England and Wales in order to secure that local government can speak with one voice. The three new associations (A.C.C., A.M.A., A.D.C.) should at least establish such a federation, if a single association is not yet practical politics. It is hoped that all the associations, together with other national local government bodies, will eventually be housed under one roof in central London.

C.L.E.A.

A Council of Local Education Authorities was formed in 1974, its members being drawn from the Education Committees of the A.C.C. and A.M.A. Its first Conference was held in Birmingham in November, 1974, and its second in Cardiff in July, 1975. Meanwhile the Association of Education Committees continues in existence, although sadly depleted in number.

THE NATIONAL ASSOCIATION OF LOCAL COUNCILS

This Association was formed in 1947, having grown out of a Parish Councils Advisory Committee of the National Council of Social Service. The new Association received a small grant from the National Council and, following the precedent of the Advisory Committee which had been founded with about a thousand affiliated parish councils, local associations had been formed in every county by 1951. There are now over six thousand parish councils in membership.

Parish councils had been abolished in Scotland in 1929 and it is thought that parish councils in England and Wales owe their survival to the patronage of the National Council of Social Service, which kept interest in them alive.

THE ASSOCIATION OF COUNCILLORS

The Association of Councillors was formed in 1963 to serve the interests of all members of local authorities. It is not, like the various local authority associations, confined to one particular class of local authority. Its other objects are to provide information and educational facilities for such members, to institute and carry on research into matters connected with local government, to exchange information and to provide a forum for discussion and to make any necessary representations. Political views of the three main parties are represented in the Association and on the controlling Court of Management, which is elected by the annual general meeting. Its headquarters are in Wiltshire.

J.A.C.L.A.P.

The Joint Advisory Committee on Local Authority Purchasing advises local authorities on such matters as organization of supplies, cleaning materials, road materials and stationery. For example, it advises the new district councils either to use the purchasing facilities of the county council or to form consortia. J.A.C.L.A.P. secretariat is provided by the local authority associations, which sponsored its formation.

The Local Government Information Office

It is convenient to conclude with an honourable mention for the Local Government Information Office, which was sponsored by the four main local authority associations. The Office performed a useful function in disseminating information on behalf of the different classes of local authority. It produced excellent leaflets (*Tomorrow's Councils, Councils for Today*) and Information Digests, but unfortunately it was a casualty of reorganization. It is pertinent to mention here the Public Relations Officer. Many authorities have now appointed such an officer, whose duties include relations with the Press, production of a civic newspaper, official guide, etc.

Local Government journals

Three weekly journals deal specifically with local government matters: *Local Government Chronicle, Local Government Review* and *Municipal and Public Services Journal.* Periodicals representing the various spheres in local government are the *County Councils Gazette*, the *Municipal Review*, the *District Councils Review* and the *Parish Councils Review*. Journals produced by professional institutes dealing partly or wholly with local government are the quarterly *Public Administration* (R.I.P.A.) and the bi-monthly *Local Government Administration* (I.L.G.A.). A monthly journal dealing with planning is the *Journal of Property and Environmental Law*, whilst the education service has *Education* and the *Times Educational Supplement*.

FURTHER READING

The local government journals cited above.

Questions

1. For what purposes are by-laws made by local authorities and who is the confirming authority?
2. What powers do local authorities possess to enable them to improve the quality of the physical environment of their areas?
3. What do you understand by the term 'injurious affection'? Link your answer with action taken following the White Paper *Development and Compensation: putting people first* (Cmnd. 5124, October 1972).
4. Examine the role and the importance of local authority associations in England and Wales. How have they been affected by the 1974 reorganization?

6 CENTRAL CONTROL

The Secretary of State for the Environment

THIS POST WAS CREATED in October, 1970, and is occupied by a leading and senior member of the Cabinet. The Secretary of State supervises a wide-ranging empire and his first task was local government reorganization, tackled on a dynamic basis for the first time this century. His responsibilities encompass housing, public health, planning and transport at a time when all these services are in the public eye.

The appointment of a Secretary of State for the Environment affords an interesting example of an application of the 'overlord' system. Formerly, the sinecure offices have been used for this purpose but without great success. The clue to real achievement in this field may well be to give the 'overlord' Minister a functional department, with specific tasks to control. The Labour government's short-lived experiment of a Secretary of State for Local Government was deficient in this respect. As forecast in the last edition, the old Ministries of Housing and Local Government and of Transport have disappeared as separate entities. The close connection between town and country planning and transport has at last been recognised. The Secretary of State is primarily concerned with the strategic issues of policy and priorities, including public expenditure. He therefore deals personally with the Department's international business, especially in Europe; environmental pollution policy; and general London policy. He is assisted in the Cabinet by the Minister for Planning and Local Government and outside it by the Minister for Housing and Construction and the Minister for Transport.

(1) THE MINISTER FOR PLANNING AND LOCAL GOVERNMENT

The antecedents of this Ministry can be tracked back to the early nineteenth century and are closely connected with public health legislation. In 1831 a Central Board of Health was established by the Privy Council to advise the local boards of health in the towns. As we know, the Poor Law Commissioners functioned from 1824 to 1847, when they were replaced by a Poor Law Board under a

President with a seat in Parliament. In 1848 a General Board of Health was set up but was not very successful, so that ten years later its powers were distributed between the Home Office and the Privy Council.

It was realized during Mr Gladstone's first Administration that the various powers of central control over local services were too diffuse; accordingly, in 1871 the Local Government Board was established under a parliamentary President. The President of the Local Government Board assimilated responsibility for the Poor Law, public health and local Acts. With the development of public health, housing and to some extent town and country planning, the President became a powerful Minister outside the Cabinet. In 1919 the Board was abolished and replaced by the Ministry of Health, the Minister having a seat in the Cabinet. The Minister of Health was responsible for poor relief, public health and general supervision of local government, including areas and finance.

In 1943 a separate Ministry of Town and Country Planning was created but this was absorbed in 1951 in a new Ministry of Housing and Local Government, which assumed responsibility for the local government functions hitherto discharged by the Ministry of Health. The Minister was responsible for environmental public services, housing, planning, new towns, water supply and local government.

The Minister for Local Government can act on behalf of the Secretary of State to confirm, modify or reject structure or local plans, to hear appeals from decisions of local planning authorities and to order public inquiries to be held in planning matters. The Secretary of State also has very wide default powers and can make a survey and development plan himself if the local authority has failed to do so. He can also order a local planning authority to acquire land for development or to secure its use in accordance with the approved plan. He is also responsible for planning matters in national parks, areas of outstanding natural beauty and surveys of rights of way. This Minister was given Cabinet status to deal with the 1974/75 Labour Government's proposals on land (the Land Community Bill).

Again, in the field of public health the Secretary of State has extensive default powers whereby he can order an inquiry into the exercise of their functions by county district councils on the complaint of a county council. He can then make an order and transfer the functions to himself or to the county council, the cost being met by the defaulting authority. In the connected area of water supply, the Minister has very wide powers. He is responsible for the appointment of members and financing of the National Water Council and

R.W.A.s (jointly with the Minister of Agriculture), and for research and publication of information on conservation of water supplies. The Minister, therefore, has wide and detailed powers in relation to local government functions, areas and finance. Although other Ministers are concerned with some local government functions, this Minister deals with all general local government problems and with compensation, land-use planning (including regional planning) outside London, the countryside, water, sewerage, refuse disposal and clean air. In all these matters the Minister acts on behalf of the Secretary of State, who also has executive power.

(2) THE MINISTER FOR HOUSING AND CONSTRUCTION

The Ministry of Public Building and Works was created in 1962, its nucleus being the old Ministry of Works which had a romantic past. In olden times it is believed that it was described as the Department of Woods and Forests. The old Ministry was confined to such matters as the preservation of ancient monuments and the maintenance of the royal parks and palaces. It thus retains responsibility for the provision, repair and maintenance of buildings for government departments; and for the royal palaces and parks and upkeep of ancient monuments and historic buildings. Its main function is to co-ordinate all building for public purposes such as housing. Its Directorate General of Research and Development in 1965 carried out a comprehensive review of research and development work related to the building and civil engineering industries. It has commissioned from the universities a number of research projects on the construction industry and has encouraged the use of the new methods of industrialized building; the grant-in-aid to the National Building Agency is mainly allotted to services given to local authorities. The Directorate of Research and Information advises on research policy and specific projects, and investigates problems connected with maintenance of buildings and use of computers in the construction industry; it also deals with training and education for the industry. It has now assumed responsibility for the Building Research Station, whose most persistent problem concerns control of noise. The main responsibilities of this Minister are for housing, including availability of land for housing; construction and building work; and the Property Services Agency, research and land use planning casework in Greater London.

(3) THE MINISTER FOR TRANSPORT

The Minister is not only responsible to Parliament for nationalized transport but also for central control of the local highway authorities, that is, for transport industries (including buses) and for transportation policy (including roads and traffic management).

The Minister can delegate repair and maintenance of trunk roads and motorways to local authorities and can resolve disputes between authorities. He may direct that a road shall be or cease to be a trunk road or motorway. The Secretary of State possesses important appellate functions under the street works code. Normally, the Minister will retain responsibility for trunk roads and motorways and he has power to construct special roads with limited access and restricted to the use of specified classes of vehicle. Existing roads can be adapted for this purpose, and both the Minister and local highway authorities can make special roads under Ministerial schemes which define the roads and the types of traffic allowed on them. This Minister is also responsible for road and vehicle safety.

The Minister for Transport may be said to share the administration of the Road Traffic Acts with the police but he can designate parking places on highways on the application of a local highway authority (except in London, where this is the responsibility of the G.L.C.). The Ministerial order will normally provide for charges to be made by parking meters.

The Minister considers draft compulsory purchase orders made by local highway authorities for road-widening schemes or other highway purposes. If objections are made, a local public inquiry may be held and the Minister, after considering the inspector's report can confirm, modify or reject the order. The Minister has power to designate Passenger Transport Authorities under the Transport Act, 1968. It must be borne in mind that, in dealing with all these functions, the Minister is acting on behalf of the Secretary of State.

The Department of Education and Science

It is possible to trace the history of the Education Department from 1839 to 1964, but here we describe the recent reorganization and upgrading of the department. The office of President of the Board of Education lasted from 1899 to 1944, when a Minister of Education with Cabinet rank was appointed. That Minister was responsible for securing the effective execution by local authorities of the national policy of providing a varied and comprehensive national education service. For twenty years the Minister of Education hovered on the brink of the Cabinet, but since 1964 a leading member of the Cabinet has been Secretary of State for Education and Science. Hitherto the Universities Grants Committee had negotiated direct with the Treasury, which otherwise had no educational responsibilities. The Secretary of State is responsible for Scottish Universities because they are financed through the Universities Grants Committee.

A Council for Scientific Policy advises the Secretary of State on national scientific needs, allocation of resources and scientific manpower. A Science Research Council encourages research in the universities and co-ordinates work on nuclear science, astronomy and space. The Industrial Research and Development Authority, the Natural Environmental Research Council and the Medical and Agricultural Research Councils also report to the Secretary of State. All these scientific responsibilities were transferred to the new Department from the office of the Lord President of the Council with responsibility throughout Britain. The Secretary of State deals with all matters which are likely to be the subject of public controversy; formulation of general policy; allocation of resources; local government reorganization as it affects the department; and international education matters. The Minister for the Arts, a Minister of Cabinet rank not in the Cabinet, assists the Secretary of State and is responsible for grants to the Arts Council and British Film Institute, government help to the crafts, national museums and galleries, national libraries (including the British Library) and public libraries.

There are a Minister of State and a Parliamentary Under-Secretary of State, one responsible for universities (throughout Britain), and for polytechnics, further education and industrial training, adult education, colleges of education, teachers and students; the other for schools, youth services, the urban programme, educational problems of immigrants and audio-visual aids in England and Wales.

A committee headed by Lady Plowden reported on primary education in all its aspects and the transition to secondary education. Plowden recommended the opening up of classrooms, a new concept of free activity teaching and greater parental integration in the running of primary schools. Many authorities, notably the I.L.E.A., have adopted these recommendations. In common with several other local education authorities, the I.L.E.A. has abolished the unpopular 'eleven-plus' examination and substituted another procedure, based on a 'primary school profile' of individual children. In July, 1965, the Secretary of State issued a circular to local education authorities asking them to submit plans for reorganizing secondary education on comprehensive lines. The plans were to provide for the integration of voluntary secondary schools into a comprehensive system in one of six main forms that have emerged so far. These include the orthodox comprehensive school with an age-range of 11–18 (the system favoured in Inner London), comprehensive schools combined with sixth-form colleges for pupils over 16 (the Leicester experiment) and a system of middle schools which straddle the primary and secondary age ranges. Statute now provides for making changes in the character, size or situation of county or voluntary schools to enable special age limits to be adopted. There was a change of policy with the change of government in 1970 so that progress towards the comprehensive system was slowed down until 1974. The Secretary of State for Wales is responsible for primary and secondary education in Wales.

The Secretary of State has very wide powers of control, including default powers, and can make regulations on such matters as maintenance of schools, standards of premises, further education and inspection. The separate departmental inspectorate is another potent instrument of control. The Minister may make an order declaring a local education authority or the governors or managers of schools to be in default and can issue directions to ensure compliance with his wishes. He can prevent the unreasonable exercise of powers by those bodies and can decide disputes between them. The Secretary of State can also hold inquiries, authorize compulsory purchase of land and confirm by-laws under the Public Libraries and Museums Act, 1964. Control is also exercised to some extent through departmental regional offices, a notable example being grant allocations under s.105 of the Housing Act, 1974.

Other Departments associated with local government

The Home Office is one of the most important of government departments for local government. It has powers to regulate the machinery of elections, and the Home Secretary is the Minister responsible for such services as the police, fire protection, and civil defence. In all these cases there is a separate Home Office inspectorate; and, the Home Secretary has wide powers under the Police Act, 1964, to order amalgamations of police forces.

Since 1965 the Welsh Department has assumed responsibility for housing, local government, land use, new towns, rent control, public health, water, civil defence and national parks in Wales. Major statutory instruments affecting England and Wales as a whole are made by the Secretary of State for the Environment in consultation with the Secretary of State for Wales. Functions relating to water, highways, bridges, forestry, tourism, ancient monuments, the Welsh language and cultural institutions in Wales have been transferred to the department.

In conclusion, we may summarize the various forms of Ministerial control over local authorities. Undoubtedly the most potent weapon is the financial one: the government grant ensures that he who pays the piper calls the tune, even if the sanction of reduction or withdrawal is hardly ever used. The role of the district auditor and the necessity for Ministerial sanction of borrowing are also relevant to financial control. Next, the power to make statutory instruments in the shape of rules, regulations or orders which are binding on local authorities is a strong weapon, assisted by circulars issued by Ministers which may be said to be of great persuasive authority since, if the advice tendered is not followed, an order can easily be made. In describing the various services we have seen the very wide default powers available to Ministers, although again they are not often used.

Ministerial confirmation, modification or rejection of by-laws, orders and schemes made by local authorities constitute another important form of control. Planning decisions and compulsory purchase orders spring to mind in this connection. In the case of certain services there are powerful inspectorates available to report to their Ministers on any maladministration or inefficiency; education and the police are the leading examples here. Certain officers can be appointed or dismissed only with ministerial approval: this applies to chief education officers, chief constables, chief fire officers and directors of social services. Finally, the different wording used by various Acts of Parliament in allocating control of a service is instructive.

The Education Act, 1944, provides that the duty of the Secretary of State is to 'promote the education of the people . . . *and to secure the effective execution by local authorities, under his control and direction*, of the national policy . . .'. A milder form of words is provided by the Local Authority Social Services Act, 1970, which provides that local authorities shall perform their functions 'under the *general guidance* of the Secretary of State'. Nevertheless the Act makes fairly drastic powers available to the Minister in other sections. Perhaps the high water-mark was reached in the Police Act, 1964, under which the Secretary of State 'shall exercise his powers . . . in such manner and to such extent as appears to him to be best calculated to promote the efficiency of the police'. The local police authority is not even mentioned and the powers of control available to the Home Secretary under the Act are certainly far-reaching. The Water Act, 1973 gives the Minister of Agriculture and the Secretary of

State for the Environment power to give water authorities directions of a general character having regard to the national policy for water and the national interest.

The Local Government Act, 1972 enables the Secretary of State for the Environment to remove or relax controls affecting the exercise of local government functions but this power has not been much exercised to date.

Examples of recent circulars

It is perhaps instructive to select at random a few recent circulars issued by D.o.E. to illustrate the wide range covered by this enormous department of State:

Provision for Sport and Physical Recreation (1/73);
Awards for Good Design in Housing 1973 (16/73);
Lorries and the Environment (57/73);
Long-distance Lorries – National Network of Secure Parks (115/73);
Urban Guideline Studies (136/73);
Local Authority Expenditure (51/75);
Publicity for the Work of Local Authorities (45/75).

The second on land availability repays careful study and follows up the White Paper *Widening the Choice: the next steps in housing* (Cmnd. 5280, April 1973, H.M.S.O.). In particular, it states that in certain circumstances extension of urban development into the countryside would be justified, although lip service is paid to green belt policy. Higher levels of residential density are also envisaged.

A circular issued jointly by D.o.E. (88/72) aad D.H.S.S. (33/72), *Heating for Elderly People in Winter*, was aimed particularly at both social services and housing authorities. Circulars issued jointly by D.o.E. and the Welsh Office (D.o.E. references given first) include:

Third Report of the Royal Commission on Environmental Pollution (118 and 264/72);
Deposit of Poisonous Waste Act, 1972 (70 and 149/72);
Lead and the Environment (6 and 6/73; 53 and 106/73);
Planning and Noise (10 and 16/73);
Publicity for Planning (71 and 134/73);
Streamlining the Planning Machine (142 and 227/73).
Land availability for Housing (102/72, 122/73).
The Public Client and the Construction Industry (53/75, 96/75)

The planning publicity circular relates to planning applications, appeals and other proposals for development and the following significant passage occurs:

> In the view of the Secretaries of State the basic principle should be that opinion should be enabled to declare itself before any approval is given to proposals of wide concern or substantial impact on the environment; and that this should be so whether the proposal is that of a government department, a local authority, statutory undertakers or a private developer.

Whoever wrote that deserves a credit mark in the annals of our democracy; and full marks to the Secretaries of State!

D.o.E. Circular 142/73 takes us a step beyond the appointment of Mr George Dobry, Q.C., an eminent planning specialist, to review the present system of development control and the arrangements for appeals. This is necessary owing to the unprecedented increase in planning applications and appeals. The circular says that planning committees should have executive powers to decide planning applications within wide terms of delegation and that greater use should be made of powers to authorize delegation to officers. The need for early submission of applications and for effective consultation is stressed. Reasons should be fully set out in the decision notice. The Development Plan Directions are being recorded and the Secretaries of State will be primarily concerned with substantial departures from structure (rather than local) plans.

In dealing with appeals, local planning authorities are urged to make fuller use of written representations procedure in lieu of a local inquiry. Streamlining of the procedure of local inquiries is also envisaged, e.g. detailed descriptions by numerous witnesses of the site can be curtailed and written statements put in. Inspectors will urge parties to be brief and to concentrate on essentials, thus avoiding repetition. This is a very important circular and it will have a lasting effect on these procedures. The circular emphazises the duty to ensure a fair hearing since it is vital that the short cuts should not imperil just decisions. Inquiries may be held in succession at one sitting lasting several days. As we go to press, Mr. Dobry's final Report has first been presented to the Secretary of State for the Environment.

Commissions for local administration

The Local Government Act, 1974 provides for setting up Commissions for Local Administration in England and Wales, on both of which the

Parliamentary Commissioner serves. Commissioners are appointed by the Crown and their chairmen selected by the Secretaries of State. At least one Local Commissioner will act for each area into which England will be divided for this purpose and a similar pattern may be extended to Wales. Local Commissioners will make annual reports to their Commissions. Representative bodies drawn from local government administration designated by the Secretary of State will receive annual reports from the Commissions.

Bodies subject to investigation comprise local authorities, joint boards, police and water authorities. Local Commissioners will investigate written complaints by individual members of the public alleging maladministration but they must relate to action taken in the exercise of administrative functions. The complaint must have been brought to the notice of the relevant local authority and it must not relate to a matter susceptible to right of appeal, reference or review to a tribunal or to remedy in a court of law. Investigation procedure is laid down in some detail (the local authority must be heard for example) and provision is made for consultation between the Local, Parliamentary and Health Service Commissioners.

FURTHER READING

J. A. G. Griffith: *Central Departments and Local Authorities* (Allen and Unwin, 1966).

J. A. G. Griffith: Local Authorities and Central Control (Local Government Review).

Questions

1. To speak of 'central control' of local government involves a misconception. It is better to speak of the 'partnership' of central and local government. Discuss.
2. What changes, if any, would you advocate in the present system of central control of local government?
3. 'Central government departments are becoming increasingly involved in the shaping of local policy.' Discuss, with particular reference to education and the personal social services.
4. Are there valid principles for determining functions and allocating them between government departments?
5. How would the political and constitutional situation of a local complaints officer be likely to differ from that of the Parliamentary Commissioner for Administration?

7 REORGANIZATION OF AREAS AND AUTHORITIES

Petition for borough status

The Local Government Act, 1972, preserves the ancient procedure of petitioning the Crown for borough status. Before 1973 an urban or a rural district council could so petition and the ultimate aim and object, though rarely achieved, was the much sought after county borough status. However, all that is water under the bridge so why should this be preserved? A borough receives a Royal Charter of incorporation and has a mayor instead of a chairman together with certain ceremonial privileges. The functions and status of the district remain the same as before in all other respects. The first step is for a resolution to be passed by a two-thirds majority at a specially convened meeting of the district council. The resolution is referred to a Committee of the Privy Council, which may then advise the Queen to grant a Charter of incorporation to the petitioning district. It should be noted that many former powerful county boroughs are now included in districts.

The abolition of existing boroughs as territorial units of local government has resulted in the lapse of pre-existing rights to borough status granted by Royal Charter, although the Charters remain and were transferred with other items such as insignia and civic plate as part of the property of the former to the new authorities. From 1974, Royal Charters will be confined to status, dignities and ceremonial; although they may confirm rights granted under earlier Charters. The grant of a Charter will ensure that the district council is reclassified as a borough council and that the chairman will become mayor. Successor parish councils based on small towns are described in the next chapter. A pre-existing borough which did not constitute the whole of a new district nor retain its separate successor parish council could petition for the grant of borough status to the district as a whole and on grant of the Charter the old borough was merged with the new borough. If no petition were lodged, charter trustees for the pre-existing area can elect one of their number as town mayor. A large borough dominating the new district could also petition for borough status. In both cases, applications had to be made to the Privy Council by the end of 1973 and about 100 charters have been issued. As the position in Wales is inextricably linked with community councils, this will be described in our next chapter.

Alteration of areas

(1) BOUNDARIES

Under the 1972 Act the Secretaries of State set up Local Government Boundary Commissions for England and Wales. Schedule 1 of the Act sets out the areas of the metropolitan counties and districts and of the shire counties but it was left to the English Boundary Commission to report on the boundaries of the new shire districts. Its Report was approved by Parliament and implemented by the Secretary of State. The Commission also advised on the establishment of successor parish councils. Comprehensive reviews of all principal local authorities in England must be undertaken by the English Commission between 1984 (ominous date!) and 1989. Meanwhile it may initiate reviews of its own accord or at the request of a local authority and must keep all shire districts under review. The Welsh Commission must undertake a special community review soon after vesting day and must continuously review all counties and districts, whose areas are set out in Schedule 4 of the Act which even includes a list of the six communities differing from the pre-existing areas. In one way the system is simpler in Wales for there are no metropolitan complications. On the other hand, the community system covers the Principality and therefore continuous reviews are necessary and may be requested. Shire districts in both countries must review parishes and communities and report to the appropriate Commission, which in turn reports to the Secretary of State. Detailed procedure is laid down in the Act, which expressly forbids promotion of local bills to alter areas.

(2) ELECTORAL AREAS

Counties are divided into electoral divisions, each returning one councillor. Districts are divided into wards and in metropolitan and some shire districts operating the system of partial renewal each ward returns a number of councillors divisible by three. Wards of shire districts having quadrennial elections return single members. A parish or community may be a single constituency or it may be divided into wards. Electoral arrangements covering boundaries and numbers of councillors are to be reviewed as a matter or urgency in 1974/75 by the Boundary Commissions (and by the districts in the case of parishes and communities). Reports must be made to the Home Secretary and the Act lays down guidelines as to ratio of councillors to electors, symmetry and identity of boundaries, number and distribution of electors and local attributes. In the case of inaction by a district council representations may be made to the Commission which can set the machinery in motion, if necessary reporting to the Secretary of State.

Functions, areas and names under the 1972 Act

The Local Government Bill, as it was then, was laid before Parliament in November 1971, and almost immediately D.o.E. Circular 84/71 listed the allocation of the main functions in England, the areas of the proposed new counties and metropolitan districts in England and the estimated populations and rateable values of the proposed counties. The county areas and names in the Bill were decided upon after consultation with local authorities. Over sixty changes were made in the proposed county area pattern and were incorporated in the Bill. Local authorities had to make proposals on the pattern of the shire districts within a fortnight of the issue of the circular. After the dinosaur-like pace of the 1958 Act procedure, this was reorganization with a vengeance! The Local Government Boundary Commission for England – Designate (as it then was) published its 'Memorandum on Draft Proposals for New Districts in the English Metropolitan Counties proposed in the Local Government Bill' in April 1972. Draft proposals for Teesside/Cleveland were published separately. The Commission were impressed by the care with which local authorities had prepared their proposals and by the extent of negotiations and discussion that had taken place between authorities. Such preparation had been undertaken almost exclusively by clerks of councils and their staffs, implementing the policy of their councils. Councils were asked to display notices, map and memorandum in their main offices for public inspection and to publish the notice in the local press for two successive weeks.

Meanwhile, time marched on, a gallant attempt was made in Parliament to give refuse disposal as well as collection to the districts but the Lords gave it back to the counties at the government's behest ('now we have it, now we don't!'), and the fateful Bill received Royal Assent on 26 October 1972. Swift as a flash came the *Local Government Boundary Commission for England Report, No. 1* (November 1972) (Cmnd. 5148) with its final recommendations for the shire districts. D.o.E. Circular 107/72 listed the areas of the new counties as laid down in the Act (shire and metropolitan, with their district areas). In December 1972, the Secretary of State (by Order laid before and approved by Parliament) gave effect without modification to the proposals in the Report. England was on the move but its slumbering

Fig. 2 Units of local government

England

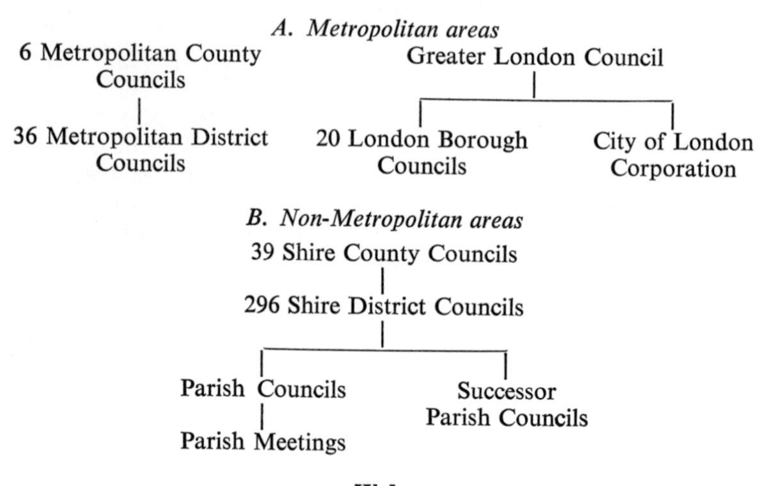

Wales

8 Shire County Councils
|
37 Shire District Councils
|
Community Councils
|
Community Meetings

citizens were not yet aware of what was happening! Thus we had the English Non-Metropolitan Districts (Definition) Order, 1972. The Circular also called for formal establishment of joint committees of the then existing authorities (see below). At the same time the Commission in Circular L.G.B.C. 1/72 issued simple guidelines for naming the new shire districts (local wishes, history, geography, simplicity, clarity). In March 1973, exactly four months after Royal Assent, the Secretary of State accepted *in toto* the recommendations of the Commission on names of the shire districts, having noted their regard for local wishes. The relevant Order came into force on 1 May 1973, just in time for the first new district council elections held on

7 June 1973. Meanwhile the Metropolitan District (Names) Order had come into force on 1 April 1973, in time for *their* elections held on 10 May 1973. The map of England was now being redrawn and the same thing was happening to Wales. The Districts in Wales (Names) Order came into operation on 31 January 1973; elections were held on 10 May 1973. The names and areas of the counties, of both types, had been delineated in the Act so that the new county elections were the first to be held, on 12 April 1973. The table below lists the local authorities in England and Wales, and a map of the authorities is included inside the back cover of this book.

It is interesting that the division of the old county of Glamorgan in Wales into three new counties caused considerable distress and, indeed, the old county advertised in the national press appealing to the public to write M.P.s to save Glamorgan from 'massacre'. The initial proposal to divide it into two new counties, East and West, had been accepted but the Secretary of State for Wales' rather late change of heart was apparently somewhat unpopular.

The New Local Authorities

A. ENGLAND – METROPOLITAN*

GREATER MANCHESTER – *Districts:* Bolton, Bury, Manchester, Oldham, Rochdale, Salford, Stockport, Tamesside, Trafford, Wigan.

MERSEYSIDE – *Districts:* Knowsley, Liverpool, St. Helens, Sefton, Wirral.

SOUTH YORKSHIRE – *Districts:* Barnsley, Doncaster, Rotherham, Sheffield.

TYNE AND WEAR – *Districts:* Gateshead, Newcastle upon Tyne, North Tyneside, South Tyneside, Sunderland.

WEST MIDLANDS – *Districts:* Birmingham, Coventry, Dudley, Sandwell, Solihull, Walsall, Wolverhamptom.

WEST YORKSHIRE – *Districts:* Bradford, Calderdale, Kirklees, Leeds, Wakefield.

B. ENGLAND – NON-METROPOLITAN*

AVON – *Districts:* Bath, Bristol, Kingswood, Northavon, Wansdyke, Woodspring.

* All metropolitan districts have been granted borough status, as have about 150 non-metropolitan districts in England and Wales.

BEDFORDSHIRE – *Districts:* Bedford, Luton, Mid Bedfordshire, South Bedfordshire.

BERKSHIRE – *Districts:* Bracknell, Newbury, Reading, Slough, Windsor and Maidenhead, Wokingham.

BUCKINGHAMSHIRE – *Districts:* Aylesbury Vale, Beaconsfield, Chiltern, Milton Keynes, Wycombe.

CAMBRIDGESHIRE – *Districts:* Cambridge, East Cambridgeshire, Fenland, Huntingdon, Peterborough, South Cambridgeshire.

CHESHIRE – *Districts:* Chester, Congleton, Crewe and Nantwich, Ellesmere Port, Halton, Macclesfield, Vale Royal, Warrington.

CLEVELAND – *Districts:* Hartlepool, Langbaurgh, Middlesbrough, Stockton-on-Tees.

CORNWALL – *Districts:* Caradon, Carrick, Kerrier, North Cornwall, Penwith, Restormel.

CUMBRIA – *Districts:* Allerdale, Barrow-in-Furness, Carlisle, Copeland, Eden, South Lakeland.

DERBYSHIRE – *Districts:* Amber Valley, Bolsover, Chesterfield, Derby, Erewash, High Peak, North East Derbyshire, South Derbyshire, West Derbyshire.

DEVON – *Districts:* East Devon, Exeter, North Devon, Plymouth, South Hams, Teignbridge, Tiverton, Torbay, Torridge, West Devon.

DORSET – *Districts:* Bournemouth, Christchurch, North Dorset, Poole, Purbeck, West Dorset, Weymouth and Portland, Wimborne.

DURHAM – *Districts:* Chester-le-Street, Darlington, Derwentside, Durham, Easington, Sedgefield, Teesdale, Wear Valley.

EAST SUSSEX – *Districts:* Brighton, Eastbourne, Hastings, Hove, Lewes, Rother, Wealden.

ESSEX – *Districts:* Basildon, Brentwood, Braintree, Castle Point, Chelmsford, Colchester, Epping Forest, Harlow, Maldon, Rochford, Southend-on-Sea, Tendring, Thurrock, Uttlesford.

GLOUCESTERSHIRE – *Districts:* Cheltenham, Cotswold, Forest of Dean, Gloucester, Stroud, Tewkesbury.

HAMPSHIRE – *Districts:* Basingstoke, East Hampshire, Eastleigh, Fareham, Gosport, Havant, New Forest, Portsmouth, Rushmoor, Southampton, Test Valley, Winchester.

HEREFORD AND WORCESTER – *Districts:* Bromsgrove, Hereford, Leominster, Malvern Hills, Redditch, South Herefordshire, Worcester, Wychavon, Wyre Forest.

HERTFORDSHIRE – *Districts:* Broxbourne, Dacorum, East Hertfordshire, Hertsmere, North Hertfordshire, St. Albans, Stevenage, Three Rivers, Watford, Welwyn-Hatfield.

HUMBERSIDE – *Districts:* Beverley, Boothferry, Cleethorpes, Glanford, Grimsby, Holderness, Kingston-upon-Hull, North Wolds, Scunthorpe.

ISLE OF WIGHT – *Districts:* Medina, South Wight.

KENT – *Districts:* Ashford, Canterbury, Dartford, Dover, Gillingham, Gravesham, Maidstone, Medway, Sevenoaks, Shepway, Swale, Thanet, Tonbridge and Malling, Tunbridge Wells.

LANCASHIRE – *Districts:* Blackburn, Blackpool, Burnley, Chorley, Fylde, Hyndburn, Lancaster, Pendle, Preston, Ribble Valley, Rossendale, South Ribble, West Lancashire, Wyre.

LEICESTERSHIRE – *Districts:* Blaby, Charnwood, Harborough, Hinckley and Bosworth, Leicester, Melton, North West Leicestershire, Oadby and Wigston, Rutland.

LINCOLNSHIRE – *Districts:* Boston, East Lindsey, Lincoln, North Kesteven, South Holland, South Kesteven, West Lindsey.

NORFOLK – *Districts:* Breckland, Broadland, Great Yarmouth, North Norfolk, Norwich, South Norfolk, West Norfolk.

NORTHAMPTONSHIRE – *Districts:* Corby, Daventry, East Northamptonshire, Kettering, Northampton, South Northamptonshire, Wellingborough.

NORTHUMBERLAND – *Districts:* Alnwick, Berwick-upon-Tweed, Blyth Valley, Castle Morpeth, Tynedale, Wansbeck.

NORTH YORKSHIRE – *Districts:* Craven, Hambleton, Harrogate, Richmondshire, Ryedale, Selby, Scarborough, York.

NOTTINGHAMSHIRE – *Districts:* Ashfield, Bassetlaw, Broxtowe, Gedling, Mansfield, Newark, Nottingham, Rushcliffe.

OXFORDSHIRE – *Districts:* Cherwell, Oxford, South Oxfordshire, Vale of White Horse, West Oxfordshire.

SALOP – *Districts:* Bridgnorth, North Shropshire, Oswestry, Shrewsbury and Atcham, South Shropshire, Wrekin.

SOMERSET – *Districts:* Mendip, Sedgemoor, Taunton Deane, West Somerset, Yeovil.

STAFFORDSHIRE – *Districts:* Cannock Chase, East Staffordshire, Lichfield, Newcastle-under-Lyme, South Staffordshire, Stafford, Staffordshire Moorlands, Stoke-on-Trent, Tamworth.

SUFFOLK – *Districts:* Babergh, Forest Heath, Ipswich, Mid Suffolk, St. Edmundsbury, Suffolk Coastal, Waveney.

SURREY – *Districts:* Elmbridge, Epsom and Ewell, Guildford, Mole Valley, Reigate and Banstead, Runnymede, Spelthorne, Surrey Heath, Tandridge, Waverley, Woking.

WARWICKSHIRE – *Districts:* North Warwickshire, Nuneaton, Rugby, Stratford-on-Avon, Warwick.

WEST SUSSEX – *Districts:* Adur, Arun, Chichester, Crawley, Horsham, Mid Sussex, Worthing.

WILTSHIRE – *Districts:* Kennet, North Wiltshire, Salisbury, Thamesdown, West Wiltshire.

C. WALES – NON-METROPOLITAN

CLWYD – *Districts:* Alyn and Deeside, Colwyn, Delyn, Glyndŵr, Rhuddlan, Wrexham-Maelor.

DYFED – *Districts:* Carmarthen, Ceredigion, Dinefwr, Llanelli, Preseli, South Pembrokeshire.

GWENT – *Districts:* Blaenau Gwent, Islwyn, Monmouth, Newport, Torfaen.

GWYNEDD – *Districts:* Aberconwy, Arfon, Dwyfor, Merionnydd, Ynys Môn (Isle of Anglesey).

MID GLAMORGAN – *Districts:* Cynon Valley, Merthyr Tydfil, Ogwr, Rhondda, Rhymney Valley, Taff-Ely.

POWYS – *Districts:* Brecknock, Montgomery, Radnor.

SOUTH GLAMORGAN – *Districts:* Cardiff, Vale of Glamorgan.

WEST GLAMORGAN – *Districts:* Afan, Lliw Valley, Neath, Swansea.

Transitional arrangements

The Rating Authorities (Initial Expenses of New Authorities) Regulations, 1973 (S.I. 1973, No. 514) required the old rating authorities to pay contributions to the respective funds of the new principal local authorities (county and district councils) 'as soon as may be after the first election of councillors'.

The Joint Committees of the pre-existing and new authorities carried out invaluable preparatory work and in Circular 50/73 D.o.E. issued guidance on such matters as preparation for the first meeting of the new councils, adoption of standing orders, committee structure, appointments of chief executives, acting clerks/secretaries and proper officers, finances, borough status, future meetings and initial postal addresses of the new councils. Emphasis was laid on publicity by the new local authorities for local government reorganization and the need to keep the public informed by means of public meetings, information in schools and delivery of leaflets. Those produced by the Local Government Information Office were very useful in this respect.

The Local Government (New Councils, etc.) Order, 1973 (S.I.

1973, No. 444) applied the Public Bodies (Admission to Meetings) Act, 1960, to meetings of the new principal authorities until vesting day (1 April 1974) after which, of course, the 1972 Act applies extending rights of admission to Committee Meetings. It also enabled their members to claim travelling, subsistence and financial loss allowances. It finally contained an important provision extending the statutory protection of an officer's terms and conditions of service to those of any officer appointed by a new authority before 1 April 1974 if he would otherwise have been transferred to that, or another, authority.

Transfer of property

Arrangements had to be made under the Act for the transfer of property from the old to the new authorities. Accordingly the Department of the Environment and the Welsh Office issued memoranda on the subject in June 1973 and the principal order transferring property from the (pre-) existing authorities to the new authorities established under the Local Government Act, 1972, and the Water Act, 1973, was laid before Parliament in November 1973. The memoranda were based on consultation papers issued by the two departments earlier in the year. The general intention, expressed in both memoranda, was to transfer all property owned immediately before they ceased to exist in 31 March 1974 by the pre-existing local authorities to the new authorities on 1 April 1974. In England, the new authorities for this purpose comprised not only the new local authorities but also the Passenger Transport Executives and the Regional Water Authorities (in Wales, also the Welsh National Water Development Authority). The Order did not generally cover property transferred to the Area Health Authorities. Such property, including school health service property, was transferred under separate statutory provision in the National Health Service Reorganization Act, 1973. Charitable trust property was automatically transferred under the 1972 Act. The memoranda laid down the general principles governing transfer of property. The most important principle was that property held by a pre-existing authority for discharge of a particular function would be transferred to the new authority which, on vesting day, would be responsible for that function and whose area incorporated that of the former authority. In the case of dual or several uses the determinant factor was the main use. 'General purpose property' was transferred to the new or 'legatee authority'; in the case of divided authorities to 'residuary legatee' authorities listed in Annex A to both memoranda.

Agency arrangements

Sections 101 and 110 of the Act provide for certain functions assigned to one type of local authority to be discharged by another type of local authority. This was enacted largely because the new district councils, although larger than their predecessors, were given much less to do in their own right. Housing was the only major service allocated outright to the shire districts and they lost functions, particularly in the fields of planning, highways, and public health. After consultation between government departments and the local authority associations, D.o.E. Circular 131/72 was issued. Examples given in the circular of functions appropriate for agency arrangements were disposal of household refuse and local aspects of road safety, training and publicity; but the bitterest battles developed over highway functions. The expertise of specialist staff, the interest of staff in their precise work location and general staffing and managerial considerations were also relevant factors. Education and social services are excluded from agency arrangements and other functions are unlikely to be susceptible to them on practical grounds, for example the fire service and strategic planning and transportation. Directions made by Ministers on agency arrangements could be made only until 31 March 1974 and remain in force only for five years thereafter. The Act provided that local authorities could apply for directions to be made and the Secretary of State then complained about the volume of applications. Decisions were issued before the end of 1973.

Highways, traffic and road safety were the subject of dispute at county/district level in a number of cases. County councils are highway authorities and district councils may maintain urban classified roads; construct and maintain footpaths and bridleways; and provide off-street car parks. The county council's highway functions are linked with those related to structure planning and promotion of public transport services. The department recognized the scope for agency arrangements, dependent to some extent on the resources of district councils in professional manpower (and the lack of it initially in the metropolitan counties). There was particularly scope for agency arrangements between the county council and districts predominantly urban and formerly possessing experienced highways or engineering departments. In the case of rural areas, where the tradition of highway maintenance is lacking, the county council could continue to act for the rural parts of the new district or could arrange for more work to be undertaken by the district council.

The department opined that there was little scope for agency in the sphere of town and country planning, although limited arrangements might be made in development control. Again, in the case of refuse disposal the need for planning over a wide area is emphasized and agency largely discounted; of course, it might have been different if disposal had gone to the districts (agency can operate in both directions). Reference is, however, made to the district incorporating a former county borough with considerable expertise and in such a case agency arrangements could be made. Further legislation is expected, following publication of the Report of the Working Party on Refuse Disposal.

In the field of consumer protection there appeared to be little scope for agency in relation to weights and measures but the protection of the public through Food and Drugs legislation affords some scope particularly having regard to hygiene. The circular is interesting on the library service in view of what subsequently happened in Wales (the responsibility is that of the Secretary of State for Education). Having argued the need for a strong county library service, it is conceded that there is scope for the larger urban shire district councils with long experience of providing comprehensive library services to undertake a range of library functions on an agency basis, where this would not impair the effectiveness of the county library service. Metropolitan district councils are library authorities and can utilize the agency provisions either with each other or with the metropolitan county acting as agent.

The conclusion of agency arrangements need not involve transfer of property to the agent authority but property could be so transferred (by agreement between the two authorities concerned) on reorganization by operation of the order. As already noted, the operation of the agency provisions has been unfortunate in some instances and U.D.C.A. complained to the Secretary of State that in some counties there had been a complete denial of agency in respect of some individual functions, such as libraries; and in others, agency had been allowed in varying degrees to some of the larger districts, normally those based on county boroughs, but denied to the remainder of the districts. Of the applications for directions 43 per cent concerned highways, 18 per cent related to consumer protection, 18 per cent to libraries, 9 per cent to planning, 9 per cent to refuse disposal and 3 per cent to miscellaneous matters.

It is fitting to pay tribute to the members and officers of local authorities up and down the country who, in spite of enormous difficulties which are not of their making, have some tremendous achievements to their credit. Leading examples of municipal enterprise are the Birmingham Municipal Bank and the local telephone service operated by the Kingston-upon-Hull Corporation. Many local authorities have played a leading part in the promotion of new universities, the key men having frequently been their town clerks or clerks.

Nor should it be forgotten that local government is an inherent part of the British system of free elections. With the advent of regional government, it is vital that local authorities should continue to represent the people on an elective basis. The problems of size, efficiency and contact with the electorate do not all lead to the same solutions. It is important that local authorities administering the personal services should not be too remote from the people; at the same time they should not be too small to be effective. There is a case for the retention of rural parishes in the counties; and there is a school of thought which advocates the creation, or re-emergence, of urban parishes.

Many other problems remain, apart from those connected with organization and structure. Perhaps Parliament could at last be persuaded to pay councillors a realistic salary. Tradition dies hard in this country. It is only comparatively recently that the concept of the professional paid politician has been accepted at Westminster.

Payment of councillors would probably attract younger people to become candidates at local elections. Much is said and written today about the declining quality of councillors. There may be an element of truth in this, but the real problem is that membership of local authorities is too often confined to retired persons, housewives, and those with private means, a rapidly dwindling class of the community. They may be, and often are, excellent people but they are hardly representative of the whole range of the population. Except in London and in some of the larger cities, the officers alone provide professional expertise.

A careful but radical reform of local government could result in a first-class service. On the whole, local government has served this country well and the new forms of organization and machinery should enable it to continue to do so.

A new claim form which will enable people to obtain up to twelve social security and local authority welfare benefits by a single application has been introduced on a trial basis in Salop.

Rent rebates or allowances, rate rebates, free school meals, and free welfare milk and vitamins are among the items covered by the form. It also caters for health service charges for prescriptions and appliances, and refunds for travelling expenses for hospital outpatients.

The single application also includes most local authority benefits available on a discretionary basis. These cover help with providing school uniform in low-income families, educational maintenance allowances, and reduced charges for some services, such as home helps and holidays for the disabled.

FURTHER READING

Local Government in England
Royal Commission 1966–1969 (Volumes I and II with maps, Cmnd. 4040, H.M.S.O.).
Government Proposal for Reorganization, 1971 (Cmnd. 4584, H.M.S.O.).
Local Government Boundary Commission for England Reports.
Local Government in Wales
Royal Commission as above.
The Reform of Local Government in Wales: Consultative Document, 1971 (H.M.S.O.).

Questions

1. 'Local government is concerned with the overall economic, cultural and physical well-being of the community.' What are the implications of this statement for the way in which a local authority is organized?
2. One of the intentions of the government in the Local Government Act, 1972, was to increase the freedom of the new local authorities in their internal management arrangements. How far has this objective been achieved and how may authorities best take advantage of the opportunities?
3. How did the Local Government Act, 1972, enable a former borough to apply for a Royal Charter? Describe the procedure and the effect of a successful application.
4. Describe the agency arrangements made possible under the Local Government Act, 1972, with particular reference to highways and libraries.

8 PARISH ADMINISTRATION

Introductory

THE ORIGIN of the civil parish can be traced back to the Statute of Highways, 1555, when local government in so far as it then existed was reorganized under the local justices of the peace with the parish or vestry as the local unit. The link with the ecclesiastical parish can be discerned in the levying of poor rates (under the Poor Relief Act, 1601) in the parishes liable also for payment of church rates. This machinery for collection was subsequently used as new local government services were introduced. Parochial officers served under the magistrates: constables, churchwardens, overseers of the poor and surveyors of highways. County matters were administered by the justices in quarter sessions. In later centuries some of these parochial functions were transferred, in some areas, to corporations for the relief of the poor and turnpike trustees. The reform of the Poor Law and other nineteenth-century reforms reduced the powers and influence of parishes and their unpaid officers, mainly because of the small size of the parish as a unit of administration. Thus the Poor Law Commissions controlled unions of parishes administered by elected guardians of the poor and this system lasted for nearly a century (1835–1930). We have seen that the late nineteenth-century reforms resulted in the Local Government Acts of 1888 and 1894, creating the local authorities as known in modern times until 1974. The 1894 Act is very important in this connection since, in the areas of the new rural districts, it created parish meetings and parish councils. The activities of the *ad hoc* boards and commissioners of the nineteenth century had encroached upon the former parochial activities and functions; this was an enlightened attempt to revive interest in local affairs in the new rural communities.

A parish meeting has been described as the only example of direct democracy in the constitution because it comprises all the local government electors for the parish. There must be an annual assembly in March and a second meeting must be held during the year if there is no parish council. If there is no parish council, the meeting chooses its chairman; otherwise the parish council chairman presides. The parish councils developed extensively in the last fifty years. Originally the civil parish had coincided with the ecclesiastical parish but only about half were identical by 1921. The formation in

1947 of the National Association of Parish Councils (now the National Association of Local Councils) led to considerable improvements in the status of parish councils and even to allocation of more functions from time to time. The Parish Councils Act, 1957, deriving in part from the old Lighting and Watching Act, 1833 (but much wider in scope, dear reviewer), is a milestone in this process. In recent years it has been apparent that the voice of parish councils has been growing more powerful, doubtless in large measure due to the strong links forged through their county branches and the national association.

There are some 8,000 parish councils but until 1974 the consent of the parish meeting was required if the parish council wished to precept for a rate of more than 1·7p, the limit being 3·3p. Meetings also controlled expenditure, housing and land disposals, whilst county councils had to acquire land compulsorily for them. Moreover, they had no right to be consulted on local planning applications. Elections were held triennially and, until 1973, rural district and parish council elections were held simultaneously and the number of councillors for each parish or ward of a parish was fixed by the county council, the electoral area being the whole parish or a ward of the parish.

Parishes in England under the Local Government Act, 1972

The pre-existing rural parishes continued in existence on 1 April 1974, when the few 'rural boroughs' created under the splendidly ponderous procedure of the Local Government Act, 1958, also continued as parishes. Parishes which were divided by the new county and metropolitan district boundaries also continue, but as separate parishes for each segment. Moreover, there must be a parish council if the number of electors in the parish is at least 200 (or at least 150 if the parish meeting so resolves, in which case the district council must establish a parish council by order). The district council may, with the consent of the parish meeting, group small parishes under one parish council, divide large parishes into wards or dissolve a parish council if the electorate is less than 150. Copies of all district council orders must be sent to the Secretary of State.

Parish councillors are now elected for four years and their number is now fixed by the district council (one of the very few powers to have been transferred from the counties to the districts!). Parish council elections were held on the same day as district council elections on 7 June 1973 and this will be the practice in future where the district council elections are quadriennial (see Table 1). A parish council must hold at least four meetings a year and elect its chairman annually. A poll of parish electors can still be demanded at a parish meeting since although the latter is open to all the local government electors of the parish, they do not all necessarily attend such meetings. Parish property is vested in the parish council or, if there is only a parish meeting, in parish trustees. Parish council functions are usually held concurrently with district councils (sometimes with county councils).

We now turn to an important and major problem under the Act, that of 'successor parish councils'. This provision is distinct from the duty of the new district councils to review parishes in their area and to make recommendations to the Local Government Boundary Commission for England.

The Act required the Commission to consult the pre-existing local authorities with a view to making proposals for the constitution and naming of parishes in the areas of former boroughs and urban districts. The Secretary of State was empowered to lay the requisite order before Parliament and this was done. Circular L.G.B.C. 1/73 laid down guidelines, the most important of which was that small towns should retain elected councils at parish levels where they are broadly comparable in size and character with other small towns or villages already having rural parish councils. But this did not include areas which were integral parts of larger towns or conurbations. Population ranges of 10,000–20,000 were set, but with some flexibility. Other factors were separate identity, history, wishes of local authorities and continuity. Applications for successor-parish council status were then invited from the former borough and urban districts qualifying under the guidelines. They have been described as the small free-standing market towns of England. The Secretary of State accepted the recommendations of the Boundary Commission (Report No. 3, H.M.S.O., 18p) and made the necessary Order designating some 170 successor parish councils. Any parish council may resolve that its area shall have the status of a town, in which case the council is the town council, the chairman becomes the mayor and the parish meeting will be the town meeting. In the case of a successor parish which was formerly a borough ownership of property and ceremonial rights will be inherited. Examples of successor parishes are Wokingham, Buckingham, Huntingdon, Gainsborough, Bodmin, Windermere, Ilfracombe. Swanage, Harwich, Epping, Cirencester, Tring, Ventnor, Sevenoaks, Oakham, Skegness, Thetford, Oundle, Hexham, Ripon, Whitby, Henley-on-Thames, Wells, Stowmarket, Godalming, Warwick, Littlehampton, Devizes and Blackrod.

Parish councils can precept on the district council for their expenses (which are chargeable on the parish) and have the power to spend up to a 2p rate for the benefit of their inhabitants. This power, coupled with the appointment of an increasing number of professional full-time parish council clerks, may well enhance the status and responsibilities of parish councils. The National Association of Local Council Clerks was formed in March 1973, and the Association has a president and other voluntary officers. New salary scales and conditions of service have been recommended.

District councils carry out reviews of parish areas and must publish their proposals which are submitted to the Local Government Boundary Commission. The Commission can hear representations, hold inquiries, reject or amend the proposals, which are then submitted to the Secretary of State, to whom further representations can be made. The Secretary of State can subsequently implement the proposals by making an Order. District councils also have power to change the name of a parish on the request of the parish council or meeting.

Property was transferred in accordance with the particular statutory purpose for which it was held. Thus property associated with concurrent powers and held by former boroughs and urban districts succeeded by parish councils was normally transferred to the latter. General purpose property related to the history or civic dignity of the town passed to the successor parish council. General office accommodation passed to the new district council in most cases and, in case of division of functions, it vested in a new authority according to balance of user of the relevant function.

Community councils in Wales

Parish government in Wales had developed on the same pattern as in England and, until 1974, there were therefore parish councils and parish meetings only in rural parishes. The 1972 Act provides for communities to be established in the whole of the Principality in the areas of former boroughs, urban districts and rural parishes and, except in six cases of divided urban districts, these old units correspond with the new communities. Community councils replace the former rural parish councils and may be established in the former urban areas by the Secretary of State for Wales; the six largest towns in Wales, however, are exempted from this provision. The Local Government Boundary Commission for Wales is charged with the duty of carrying out a special community review in Wales as soon as practicable after vesting day (1 April 1974).

There is permissive power for a community meeting comprising all the local government electors to be convened and for it to elect a chairman for the meeting. The district council must establish a community council at the behest of a community council which is not identical with the district; this would appear to relate only to the rural and the split urban areas. The district council must also dissolve the community council at the request of the community meeting. Community councillors will in future be elected for four years but those elected in 1974 hold office until 1979. A community council elects a chairman and must meet at least once a year. In all other respects the Welsh Community Councils and meetings operate on the same basis as the English parish councils and meetings and exercise the same functions. Property of a pre-existing parish was transferred to the new community council, where there was one, or to the new district council if there was not. The vesting of property was arranged on the same lines as in England but with certain differences, having regard to the establishment of communities throughout Wales and the creation of successor parish councils in England. The general effect is that the situation is rather more straightforward in Wales with a simple choice between the district and the community council in most cases. Examples of communities in Wales are Colwyn Bay, Prestatyn, Llandudno, Montgomery, Radnor, Brecon and Carmarthen.

Functions and finance in England and Wales

Parish and community councils have the same functions and these are set out in the accompanying list. They also have the right to be consulted about planning applications affecting land in their areas and to appear at public inquiries even if there is no direct legal interest. This is an example of the public participation in the planning process advocated in the Skiffington Report in 1969. Parish and community councils can also provide conference facilities and provide or encourage tourism, arts and crafts and public entertainment.

List of Parish and Community Council Functions

Museums*	Footway lighting*
Parks and open spaces*	Parking (cycles and motor-cycles)
Swimming baths*	Off-street parking*
Physical training and recreation*	Bus shelters
Village greens	Roadside seats

Village halls and community centres	Traffic signs
Parish and community buildings	Allotments*
Public clocks	Grass verges
Public conveniences*	Closed churchyards
Wash houses and launderettes	Burial grounds
Footpaths and bridleways* (Maintenance and sign-posting)	Cemeteries and crematoria*
	Unclaimed land

* Powers exercised concurrently by district councils.

Parish and community councils issue precepts to their rating authorities and their expenses are chargeable in their respective parishes or communities. A county council may contribute towards certain expenses as special expenses, for example the cost of provision of public open spaces. Moreover, two or more local authorities may make arrangements to defray expenditure incurred in the exercise of concurrent functions.

If a successor parish council decides to provide a swimming pool or a playing field, the cost would fall on the parish unless such an arrangement were to be made. The expenses of providing these facilities elsewhere in the district would be chargeable over the whole area. This would include the parish which had itself provided its own facilities. The alternative method would be for the district to charge the expenses as special expenses relating to the other part of the district enjoying the benefit of the facilities. Expenditure would normally be charged over the whole area of the district authority since the power to charge special expenses is exercised sparingly.

FURTHER READING

Arnold-Baker, C.: *New Law and Practice of Parish Administration* (Longcross Press, 1969).

Questions

1. 'Public participation in local authority decision-making brings both costs and benefits.' Discuss.
2. Do you think that the parishes and communities are sufficiently representative of the 'grass-roots'? Give reasons for your answers.
3. What are successor parish councils? Describe their constitution, powers and functions.

9 GREATER LONDON

'London, thou art the flower of cities alle . . .'

Historical introduction

SPECIAL PROBLEMS of organization and administration have always been present in the metropolis owing to its position as the seat of government and capital of the country. These were accentuated by the great size of London, in terms both of area and population, which in turn necessitated urgent attention being given to sanitation. By 1830 there were eight separate bodies of Commissioners of Sewers for London and these were unified in 1848 into one new body of Commissioners of Sewers for the Metropolis.

In 1834 the parish vestries (based on ecclesiastical divisions), lost their Poor Law functions to the new boards of guardians but the special public health problems of London led Parliament to create numerous 'select vestries' (as opposed to 'open vestries'), in some of which the vestrymen were popularly elected if the parish availed itself of adoptive legislation. In some parts of the Metropolis Parliament provided for the creation of district boards governing two or more small parishes. Both the metropolitan vestries and district boards received powers in such matters as highways and sanitation which elsewhere later became the functions of *ad hoc* boards. By the middle of the nineteenth century the metropolitan vestry had become the normal unit of local administration.

However, there was no general control over this great conglomeration of vestries and boards. Accordingly, the Metropolis Management Act of 1855 reorganized the parochial vestries and district boards in London and transferred to them the powers of the former paving commissioners. London for this purpose comprised the area subsequently administered by the L.C.C. from 1889 to 1965. This Act, a vital landmark in the history of London local government, also set up the Metropolitan Board of Works comprising forty-six members elected by the vestries and district boards. The new Board was responsible for main drainage and bridges throughout the metropolis and also exercised certain improvement powers. In 1866 the Metropolitan Fire Brigade (renamed the London Fire Brigade in 1904) came into existence and was placed under the control of the Metropolitan Board of Works.

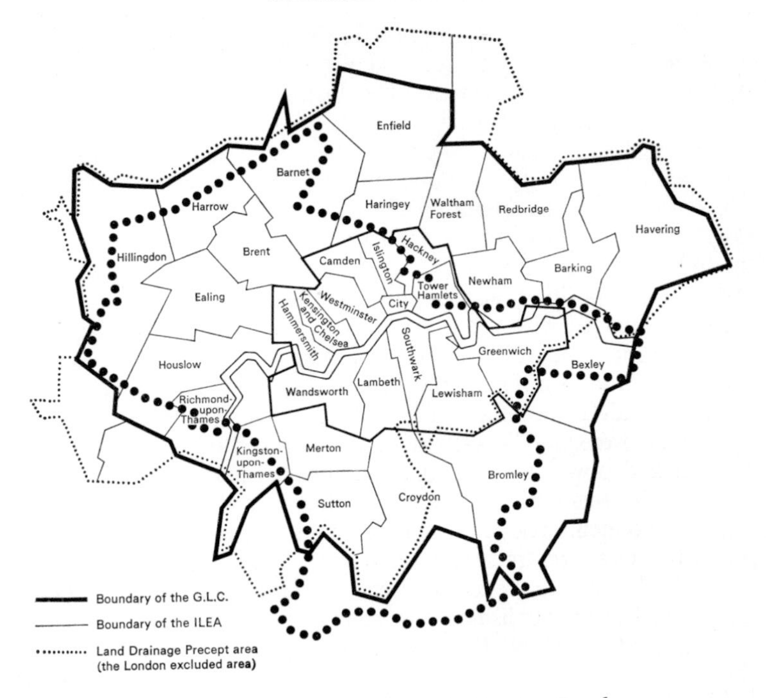

Fig. 3 Administrative areas in Greater London

City of London Corporation

12 Inner London Boroughs

CAMDEN
GREENWICH
HACKNEY
HAMMERSMITH
ISLINGTON
KENSINGTON AND CHELSEA
LAMBETH
LEWISHAM
SOUTHWARK
TOWER HAMLETS
WANDSWORTH
WESTMINSTER CITY

20 Outer London Boroughs

BARKING
BARNET
BEXLEY
BRENT
BROMLEY
CROYDON
EALING
ENFIELD
HARINGEY
HARROW
HAVERING
HILLINGDON
HOUNSLOW
KINGSTON-UPON-THAMES
MERTON
NEWHAM
REDBRIDGE
RICHMOND-UPON-THAMES
SUTTON
WALTHAM FOREST

The closing years of the nineteenth century witnessed notable local government reforms, not least in London, which were to endure for well over half a century. The Local Government Act, 1888, abolished the Board, replacing it with the London County Council, which came into existence the following year. The L.C.C. differed in material respects from the other county councils created by the Act, since the latter were based on the ancient geographical counties of England and Wales. The L.C.C. was carved out of the urban or metropolitan areas of the counties of Middlesex, Surrey and Kent. Its internal composition was broadly the same as that of the other county councils, with some exceptions. Thus it had a chairman, a vice-chairman, aldermen and councillors, all the latter and one-half of the total number of aldermen having been elected triennially. However, the aldermen, although holding office for the usual period of six years, were only one-sixth of the number of councillors. The L.C.C. had power to appoint a deputy chairman and the practice was to offer this position to a leading member of the minority party on the council. The electoral divisions were the parliamentary constituencies, each returning three councillors.

The London Government Act, 1899, took the reorganization a stage further by abolishing the metropolitan vestries and district boards and replacing them with twenty-eight new metropolitan borough councils. Unlike the borough councils outside London which had been incorporated by Royal Charter, the metropolitan borough councils were purely creatures of statute and did not receive Charters. Each metropolitan borough council annually elected a mayor and triennial elections were held of councillors and one-half of the number of aldermen, the latter being one-sixth of the number of councillors. As in the rest of the country, the aldermen were drawn from the councillors or persons qualified to be councillors and, once elected, served for six years, one-half of their number retiring every three years. Thus the aldermanic system, entrenched in the municipal boroughs, was extended not only to the new county councils but also throughout London, albeit on a narrower basis.

The L.C.C. was the local authority responsible throughout the area of the old County of London for education, town planning and main drainage, it also administered the personal health, welfare and child care services. Nine administrative divisions controlled from County Hall administered certain local aspects of education, health and welfare (I.L.E.A. now has 10 education divisions). For example, the education divisions serviced the governing and managing bodies of schools by providing clerks to the governors and managers. Local co-ordination of services could also be effected: for example the divisional education officer would consult the divisional medical officer on the school health service or the area children's officer on problem children. The L.C.C.'s Junior Leaving Examination, popularly known as the 'eleven-plus examination', was administered locally in the divisions, which provided Clerks to the Local Advisory or Selection Committees. Maintenance and uniform grants and free travel passes for secondary school children were also obtainable through the divisional offices.

Some planning functions were delegated to the metropolitan borough councils, but there was a special delegation scheme in the case of the City of London. As regards the exercise of local government functions, the City Corporation was more or less in the position of a metropolitan borough with special privileges. The L.C.C. did not control main roads or the police, the metropolitan borough councils having been the local highway authorities for all except major roads. The metropolitan borough councils were responsible in their areas for housing, public health (administration of by-laws, including those made under the London Building Acts; sewers, sanitation, clean air zones, food and drugs legislation), rating and libraries. Both the L.C.C. and the metropolitan borough councils had concurrent housing powers in relation to slum clearance and the provision of new housing. Thus the main differences between local administration in the County of London and the counties elsewhere were, on the one hand, the concurrent housing powers in London (an ordinary county council having only very limited housing powers for overspill purposes) and, by contrast, the greater responsibilities vested in the metropolitan borough councils for highways. There was also special legislation for London, notably in the case of public health.

The London Government Act, 1963

Certain parts of Hertfordshire and Surrey originally included in the Review area were excluded from the area administered by the G.L.C. which is known as Greater London. This is defined as the area comprising the London boroughs, the City of London and the Inner and Middle Temples. One hundred councillors (one for each Parliamentary constituency in the area) and sixteen aldermen were elected in April, 1964, the first general election of councillors for the G.L.C. The new council elected a Chairman, Vice-Chairman and Deputy-Chairman from its members, the last-named post being offered to a representative of the minority party, in accordance with the traditional practice of the L.C.C. Elections are held triennially.

The first London borough council elections were held in May

1964. Responsibility for the administration of relevant functions and certain assets and property vested in the G.L.C. and the L.B.C.s respectively on 1 April 1965. The pre-existing authorities in Greater London expired on 31 March 1965. Thus the old authorities co-existed with the new for the better part of twelve months. The first meetings of the new authorities were held swiftly following the elections in 1964 to enable appointments to be made of chief officers, deputy chief officers and general administrative, professional, technical and clerical staff. Under the Local Government Act, 1972, the Aldermen will disappear in 1976 (G.L.C.) and in 1977 (L.B.C.s). The Secretary of State is empowered to order quadrennial elections in Greater London and to introduce the system of partial renewal in the London Boroughs.

The Act enabled the Queen-in-Council to grant charters of incorporation of the inhabitants of a London borough, following representations by the Minister of Housing and Local Government to the Privy Council. This was done in each case and in 1964 the Minister made orders naming the boroughs following representations by joint committees of the old authorities. Thus although the London boroughs are creatures of statute, they have been granted Royal Charters. The reason for this is that, whereas the old metropolitan boroughs and urban districts in the area were statutory, the county boroughs and non-county boroughs were all incorporated by Charter. It was therefore appropriate to issue Royal Charters to all the new boroughs, whatever the status of their various predecessors-in-title may have been. The expression 'Inner London' refers to the old L.C.C. area; 'Outer London' means the remainder of Greater London.

Functions of the G.L.C. and L.B.C.s

In general it should be noted that, except where otherwise indicated, the G.L.C. has the same powers as metropolitan county councils under the Local Government Act, 1972, and the L.B.C.s have the same powers as metropolitan district councils. The most important exception to this general principle relates to education administration. Education in the former County of London is the responsibility of the Inner London Education Authority, whose members comprise the G.L.C. members for Inner London and representatives from the City Corporation and from each of the twelve Inner London Boroughs. The I.L.E.A. is described in the 1963 Act as a special Committee of the G.L.C. and it has control over the appointment of its officers, except in so far as it is subject to the general rule that the appointment of a chief officer must be approved by the Secretary of State. The I.L.E.A. also determines the amount of the G.L.C.'s education precept levied on the rating authorities in Inner London. For these reasons, the I.L.E.A. would appear to be in the position of an *ad hoc* authority for education in Inner London. The G.L.C. has no option but to precept for the amount required by the I.L.E.A., whose independent position is analogous to that of a county police committee.

The twenty Outer London Borough Councils are local education authorities in their own right. This is logical, because many of the Outer London Boroughs have been formed from amalgamations of 'excepted districts'.

The effect of the Local Authority Social Services Act, 1970, was that all the L.B.C.s became the social services authorities throughout Greater London. As they are also housing authorities, the Seebohm doctrine has been implemented in London. A London Boroughs Training Committee (Social Services) co-ordinates the training of social workers.

The G.L.C. is the local planning authority for Greater London and is responsible for the preparation of a structure plan for the area but the L.B.C.s must prepare local plans and have certain planning functions. The G.L.C. may prepare a local plan for the whole or part of a G.L.C. action area jointly with an L.B.C. Except for the reception of applications for planning permission, which remains the function of the borough councils, the G.L.C. is the local planning authority for the three main types of development. With certain exceptions it is the planning authority for areas of Comprehensive Development in Inner London; for certain specified classes of development relating mainly to large buildings; and for certain applications for the extraction of minerals.

The Greater London Development Plan was published in 1969 and has since been the subject of an inquiry by an independent panel who have submitted their report to the Secretary of State. On approval, the Plan will be treated as a structure plan under the new planning system. Its main elements embrace population and housing, employment and transport but it also deals with the use of the Thames, public open space, the Green Belt, education, shopping, markets, public utilities and tourism. The Plan identifies special areas requiring protection and fifty-six action areas ripe for comprehensive redevelopment. Plans for most of the action areas will be prepared by the L.B.C.s but the G.L.C. is involved in large schemes such as Thamesmead, Covent Garden and Dockland. L.B.C.s must seek directions of the G.L.C. before granting permission relating to major shopping developments, high buildings, substantial office or industrial schemes, developments affecting metropolitan roads, traffic and transport, Green Belt, works to buildings of architectural or historic interest and proposals departing substantially from the Initial Development Plan. Thus the G.L.C. deals with applications relating to large concert halls, stadia, university buildings, airports and railway termini and its own comprehensive development areas.

The L.B.C.s are the local housing authorities or the 'primary units for housing'; they therefore have all necessary powers under the Housing Acts. However, the G.L.C. also has power to provide new housing accommodation both inside and outside Greater London, but it must in general obtain the consent of the L.B.C. if it wishes to build within the area of that borough. For the time being, until such date as the Minister may appoint, the G.L.C. may exercise certain other housing powers concurrently with the L.B.C.s but it cannot deal with abatement of overcrowding or houses in multiple occupation. Under the London Government Act, 1963, the G.L.C. housing estates can be transferred by agreement to the L.B.C.s; and the Secretary of State has power to direct such transfer by order. The first stage of handing over the estates to L.B.C.s has commenced. The G.L.C. maintains a record of need and facilities for the exchange of housing accommodation and the L.B.C.s maintain housing registers. The aim is for the G.L.C.'s central record to be continuously supplied with information from the L.B.C.s. The G.L.C. maintains and manages its stock of 200,000 homes (management being decentralized to district offices), modernizes and rehabilitates older dwellings and provides homes for Londoners outside London in the expanding and new towns. As the regional strategic authority, the G.L.C. cooperates closely with the L.B.C.s on housing policy and, in particular, shares in slum clearance in Inner London and helps to maintain the rented sector by a programme of purchase. It also helps to provide new dwellings needed both to make good the housing shortage and to replace homes demolished for roads and schools. A comprehensive survey of its stock of older houses is under way with a view to modernization. The G.L.C. has provided over 1,000 bungalows and flats for old people in seaside towns. Its home loan scheme has been overtaken by inflation.

In 1964 the Milner Holland Report disclosed some appalling facts about housing in London and indicated that no policy for housing in London could be formed unless the necessary facts were available. L.B.C.s alone maintain waiting lists in London. Qualifications to get on an L.B.C.s waiting list are now uniform and such flexibility is invaluable in view of the gross overcrowding in some

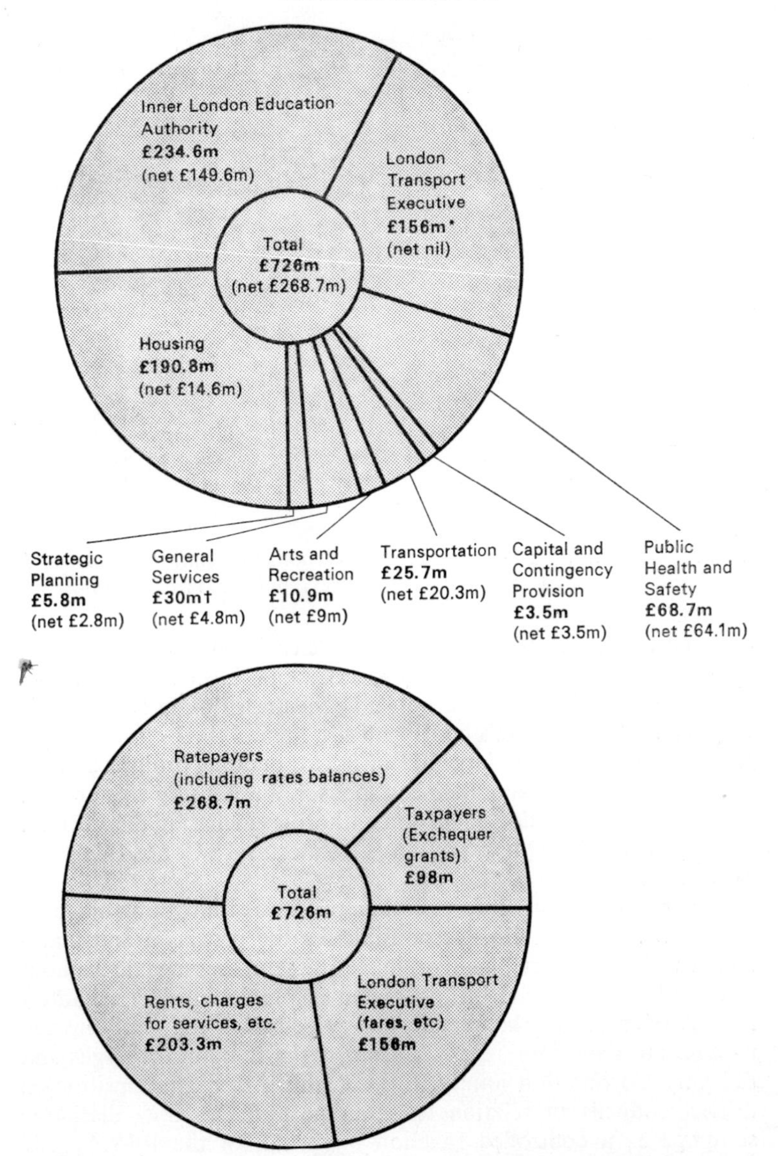

Fig. 4 G.L.C., I.L.E.A. and L.T.E. gross revenue expenditure in 1973–74 and how it was to be met (from 'Greater London Services 1973–74')

* Estimated revenue expenditure during 1973.
† Excludes £37.2m on behalf of the I.L.E.A. included in the I.L.E.A. total.

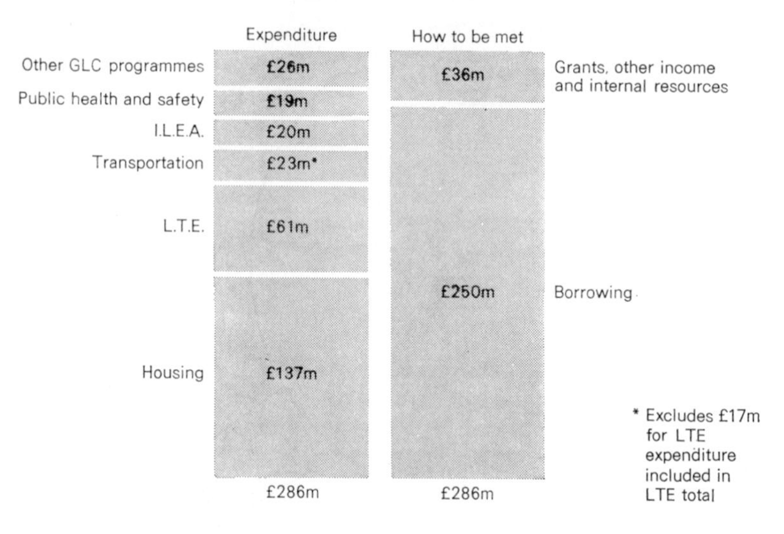

Fig. 5 G.L.C., I.L.E.A. and L.T.E. gross capital expenditure in 1973–74 and how it was to be met (from 'Greater London Services 1973–74')

boroughs. The G.L.C. also operates a 'clearing-house' to facilitate exchanges of dwellings between G.L.C. and L.B.C. tenants. The concept of priority neighbourhoods under the Housing Act 1974, is very relevant to London's housing needs. Some L.B.C.s have formed groups to carry through large industrialized building projects and the London Boroughs Committee has sponsored a housing consortium. Over half of the London education authorities including the I.L.E.A. have joined the Metropolitan Architectural Consortium for Education.

The L.B.C.s must enforce certain public health by-laws made by the G.L.C. The G.L.C. is responsible for the provision and maintenance of main sewers, main drainage and land drainage throughout Greater London. The G.L.C. is treated as a regional water authority for the purposes of the Water Act, 1973, and it may appoint ten members to the Thames R.W.A., as may the London Boroughs and the City Corporation jointly. L.B.C.s are in the same position as district councils in relation to sewerage and can now discharge sewerage as a controlled function on behalf of the R.W.A. The indestructibility of some aspects of the old L.C.C. administration is illustrated by the fact that it has proved impossible to dislodge the London Building Acts. Accordingly, the Building Regulations, 1972, which apply to the rest of England and Wales, do not apply to Inner

London, which retains its separate building code. The L.B.C.s are responsible for refuse *collection* and other public health matters; the G.L.C. arranges refuse *disposal*. This pattern has been followed in the rest of the country.

In the case of highways, there is a new classification of 'metropolitan roads' (including principal roads) for which the G.L.C. is responsible. This is closely linked with traffic engineering and management and the G.L.C. has a Department of Planning and Transportation. Opposition is growing to the current proposals for motorway boxes on both sides of the river; in addition, the Archway Road (A1–M1 spur) road widening scheme ran into much local opposition channelled by the Archway Road Campaign. It has at last been completed, after years of desolation. The destruction of good housing accommodation and consequential displacement of residents seem too high a price to pay for smooth traffic flow, whose increased speed brings danger to young and old alike.

The L.B.C.s are responsible for the maintenance of 'non-metropolitan' roads, in other words all highways except trunk roads. The G.L.C. has a general duty in relation to road traffic and has powers to make traffic regulation orders and experimental traffic schemes, and to provide parking accommodation, concurrently with L.B.C.s, and traffic signs. Thus the Christmas shopping parking arrangements for central London and restrictions on off-street parking now emanate from the G.L.C. The G.L.C. is responsible for making schemes for pedestrian crossings on all roads in its area other than the trunk roads.

The G.L.C. is responsible for the broad policy and financial control of the Underground and central bus services administered by L.T.E. (see below); and for construction, maintenance and lighting of all main roads (except trunk roads) in its area. Its role as strategic planning authority for Greater London can be clearly discerned, for example by co-ordination of transport planning. The Intelligence Unit set up under the 1963 Act is now in the Department of Planning and Transportation and collates information for the benefit of local authorities, government departments and the public. It has a special division to undertake work on behalf of the London Boroughs. Examples of the Department's recent innovations include computer control for traffic signals, severe parking restrictions and the banning of heavy lorries from certain areas.

The G.L.C. is responsible for the London Fire Brigade. It precepts upon the L.B.C.s, which are the local rating and library authorities and the main civil defence authorities. The accounts for both the G.L.C. and the L.B.C.s are subject to district audit (or approved audit if the appropriate resolution is passed under the Local Government Act, 1972). The London Boroughs Committee and the London Boroughs Management Services Unit co-ordinate action on matters of common interest.

The new authorities in action

The new authorities have been exercising their functions for a decade and some illustrations of their achievements follow.

INNER LONDON

The I.L.E.A. during the first year of its existence abolished the Junior Leaving Examination (the 'eleven-plus exam') and replaced it by a system of free parental choice. During each child's last year at primary school a 'profile' of his or her work is compiled from gradings of the Head and the results of verbal reasoning tests. Overall assessments of standards are checked centrally against tests taken in all schools. The parent chooses a school for his offspring in consultation with the primary school Head and the profiles are available to secondary Heads.

The success of the scheme will probably greatly ease the Inner London transition to fully comprehensive education since school neighbourhood zones or catchment areas should not be necessary. Parental choice can range over single-sex and co-educational schools, large or medium sized schools, 'aided' or 'county' schools. Other local education authorities are seeking detailed information from the I.L.E.A., which emphasizes the parent–teacher relationship and the traditions, inherited from the L.C.C., of trying to meet parental wishes. At present the scheme embraces direct-grant, aided and maintained grammar schools; and comprehensive schools. But even when the authority's area is fully comprehensive some schools will have different specialities, such as technology, and others will have an academic bias. All children in London secondary schools can follow courses most suited to their needs and talents. Grammar and comprehensive schools provide a variety of sixth form options. Arrangements are sometimes made with neighbouring schools and colleges for specific options. Special tuition is available in reception classes for children with little or no English and for children with special difficulties. In 1974 I.L.E.A. established some much smaller comprehensive schools with rolls of about 450 each.

LAMBETH

In 1971 Lambeth L.B.C. opened a Housing Advisory Centre next to the Town Hall. The new Housing Advisory Service was established primarily to help all members of the public with housing problems. A team of specialist officers assembled under one roof can give advice on loans, mortgages, house purchase, improvement grants, rehabilitation of old houses, rehousing, rents, housing outside London, disrepair in the private sector and guidance to those facing eviction. An efficient appointments system in an attractive office building enables specialists to answer questions and advise on the spot. The Government Rent Officers are located in the same building, and the Council's Environmental Health Inspectorate, Borough Valuer and Housing Management Department are all housed within adjacent offices to provide a fully integrated service.

A Research and Development team advises on housing need in the Borough whose housing requirements are being fostered by assessment of relevant information, intelligent use of existing housing stock, arrest of decay by means of Housing Action Areas, environmental improvements and redevelopment. Lambeth L.B.C. identify four main objectives:

1 to solve the problem associated with housing in the minds of the public;
2 to make the best possible use of existing housing stock:
3 to preserve the socio-economic balance of the neighbourhood; and
4 to attract landlords to modernize structurally sound older houses into new homes with modern amenities.

HOUNSLOW

In 1966, the London Borough of Hounslow announced an imaginative plan to revitalize Brentford, the former county town of Middlesex and one of the oldest towns in Britain. Under the plan Brentford, much of which is derelict or decaying, will become an attractive town, making far greater use of its Thames-side position. The proposals, involving about 400 acres south of the Great West Road, include ambitious housing developments, a 'town quay', a footbridge over the Thames to link with Kew Gardens, a boating lake, an educational and cultural centre and a riverside walk to the World Garden Centre at Syon Park. It will take about twenty years to implement the scheme; the large-scale housing development, however, has started and the high-rise housing scheme has been completed, the first tenants being now in occupation. A further instalment of low-rise housing and a scheme for housing the elderly are under construction. Consultation has taken place between the local authority and interested bodies such as the four local preservationist societies. Public reaction and comment is a key feature in the adoption of the blue-print for 'New Brentford'.

TOWER HAMLETS

(1) *Isle of Dogs*

A circular issued by the Department of Education and Science in 1970 to local education authorities suggested that there might be economic and social advantages in providing welfare and recreation amenities as part of a school complex. This idea was taken up in respect of the George Green School being built by the Inner London Education Authority on the Isle of Dogs in the London Borough of Tower Hamlets. As a result and with co-operation between the I.L.E.A., the borough council and the government departments concerned, the school complex contains a day nursery, an old people's day centre and an area social service office, paid for by the borough council. Shared facilities which will be paid for jointly in proportion to their use by the borough council and the I.L.E.A., include a sports hall, a bar lounge, games areas and changing rooms. The day nursery provides fifty places and the day centre caters for about eighty elderly and handicapped persons. It is intended to incorporate a luncheon club and to serve meals through the school kitchen. Users of the day centre will be able to participate in the facilities offered by the school, particularly the instructional and recreational facilities offered by adult education. A centre manager with supporting staff will manage the shared complex and he will be responsible to a Management Committee comprising representatives of the borough council and the I.L.E.A. There will also be a consultative Committee comprising locally involved officers such as the Headmaster, the Senior Youth Officer, the Principal of the Adult Education Institute, together with borough officers and a member of the Sports Council to advise on the day-to-day running of the centre. The school and complex is due to be completed by September 1975. This affords an excellent example of co-operation between D.E.S., D.H.S.S., I.L.E.A. and the L.B.C.

TOWER HAMLETS

(2) *Spitalfields*

In 1968 the L.B.C. made a compulsory purchase order under Part III of the Housing Act, 1957, on some 700 dwellings in tenement blocks which were unfit for human habitation. At that time, this was one of the largest C.P.O.s of this nature made in the London area. It was confirmed in 1970 and rehousing was expected to take five years. Redevelopment to a lower density is expected to commence in 1975.

The L.B.C. were thus able to deal with a very heavily populated area in a comparatively short space of time.

G.L.C.

The Thamesmead Committee, which includes representatives of the Greenwich and Bexley L.B.C.s, is responsible for building Thamesmead, an entirely new community on the site of the former Royal Arsenal at Woolwich and Erith Marshes. Some 2,000 families are already in occupation and another 2,500 homes are under construction. Eventually nearly 15,000 people will be accommodated. Industrial development is proceeding apace to provide employment. Thamesmead will have a river frontage of over three miles and a network of lakes, canals, a marina and open space with emphasis on environmental qualities. Paths and elevated walkways linking homes, shops, schools and parks segregate pedestrians from traffic. Social flexibility will be ensured by variety in housing, schools, shops, offices, factories and amenities for all age groups. H.M.G., G.L.C., I.L.E.A., Bexley and Greenwich L.B.C.s jointly share public investment in the project amounting to about £150m.

London Transport

The Transport (London) Act, 1969, imposes a general duty on the G.L.C. to develop policies and to encourage, organize and carry out measures to promote the provision of integrated, efficient and economic transport in Greater London. To this end the G.L.C. must prepare plans relating to transport in Greater London and send copies to the Minister after consultation with him, B.R.B., L.T.E. and affected local authorities.

The Act provided for the constitution of a London Transport Executive comprising a chairman appointed by the Council and not less than four nor more than ten other members appointed by the Council after consultation with the chairman. All members must be appointed from persons with wide experience and capacity in transport, industry, commerce or finance, administration, applied science or the organization of workers. L.T.E. has power to pay its members salaries, fees and allowances to be determined by the G.L.C. Provision is also made for pension rights and compensation for loss of office. Powers are conferred directly on the L.T.E., which is responsible for day-to-day operations and management.

The L.T.E., B.R.B. and National Bus Company must co-operate for the purpose of co-ordinating and providing effective passenger transport services. L.T.E. must promote and utilize research and the G.L.C. may give it directions. L.T.E. is given wide powers to carry passengers by road, rail and water. The Act provides for notification by B.R.B. to G.L.C. of proposed railway closures and for a procedure enabling G.L.C. to protest to the Minister. G.L.C. has set up an independent London Passengers' Transport Committee.

L.T.E. must prepare an annual statement of audited accounts and an annual report for the G.L.C. and send a copy to the Minister. G.L.C. has power to give general directions to the L.T.E. on financial matters, including estimates, proposals for substantial outlay on capital account and the general level and structure of fares (to be charged to bus and rail passengers), which must be published if G.L.C. so direct. Provision is made for consultation on fares between G.L.C. and local authorities, which must be informed in advance of any proposed change of substance. G.L.C. is empowered to review the L.T.E.'s organization and to give relevant directions and has directed L.T.E. to balance its revenue account in 1973 and in later years. G.L.C. makes grants to L.T.E. towards such projects as the new Fleet underground line and the Piccadilly Line extension to Heathrow. L.B.C.s have power to arrange concessionary fare schemes with L.T.E. for blind, disabled and elderly people.

The City of London

The City of London Corporation, which is a body corporate by prescription or custom, remains unreformed and has done rather well out of the reorganization, since it has acquired more functions. The Lord Mayor is Admiral of the Port of London and Lord Lieutenant of the City. The Court of Common Hall comprises the Lord Mayor, sheriffs, aldermen and freemen of the City. As the City of London is also technically a separate county, Common Hall enjoys the privilege of annually electing the two City sheriffs. It also nominates two senior aldermen for the election of one as Lord Mayor by the Court of Aldermen, which also elects the Recorder of the City of London. Aldermen of the City of London are elected for life and *ex officio* can sit alone as justices of the peace. Nowhere else in the country can lay justices sit alone.

The Court of Common Council is the real governing body of the City Corporation and comprises the Lord Mayor, twenty-six aldermen and 159 common councilmen, who can perhaps best be described as 'uncommon councillors'. The Common Council controls the property of the Corporation and maintains Tower, London, Southwark, and Blackfriars Bridges over the Thames. Thus the cost of rebuilding London Bridge at a sum exceeding £2 million was met from the Committee's funds and none of it was borne by the general taxpayer or ratepayer. The Common Council retains the functions formerly discharged in common with the metropolitan borough councils: housing, public health, highways, rating and libraries. In addition, it remains the port health authority for the Port of London. Under the new dispensation, the Common Council is responsible for social services; and for non-metropolitan roads. This is because, under the 1963 Act, whilst the internal composition and structure of the City Corporation are untouched, it exercises all the functions of a L.B.C.

There is a close link between the City Corporation and the ancient City livery companies, such as the Mercers, the Haberdashers, the Brewers and the Apothecaries. Some of the liverymen of the City companies are also free of the City. As Sir William Hart, the distinguished former Clerk of the G.L.C., says in his book (*Law of Local Government and Administration*), 'The City Corporation remains a picturesque and honourable relic of a former state of society, and is important not so much because of its local government activities as of its charitable work, the positions of high dignity which it can offer its members and the honourable hospitality it can give to distinguished visitors from other countries.'

The ancient traditions of the City Corporation are reflected to some extent in the titles of its chief officers. Whilst it has a town clerk (itself an appellation of no mean ancestry), there are also a City Solicitor and Controller, a City Chamberlain (who performs the office of a treasurer) and a City Remembrancer. Although the City Corporation is not a local education authority it maintains the City of London schools; and many of the numerous London voluntary-aided schools furnish a working partnership between the City Companies, who provide the governing bodies and much of the cash required, and the local education authority. All these schools are now located outside the City of London with one exception. The governors of voluntary aided schools receive a departmental grant of 80 per cent of their proportion of the cost of alterations and repairs. At the same time, the City Corporation keeps up to date, for example in its participation in the imaginative Barbican housing development scheme.

Special *ad hoc* authorities for London

We should mention that the Home Secretary, acting through a Commissioner of Police, is the police authority in the Metropolitan Police District; and that there is a separate police force in the City of London, for which the City Corporation is responsible. These arrangements differ substantially from those obtaining in the rest of the country in respect of police forces. The Royal Commission did not examine police functions in Greater London, nor was the metropolitan administration of the police disturbed by the Police Act, 1964.

The Metropolitan Water Board was constituted under the Metropolis Water Act, 1902, to administer the supply and distribution of water in a large area of what is now Greater London. The Metropolitan Water Board is a highly efficient undertaking and has even managed, on occasion, to *reduce* the water rate once or twice since the war. Its reward has been to be incorporated in the Thames R.W.A. as its Metropolitan Water Division.

The Port of London Authority was created in 1909 and controls the Port of London, reaching to Teddington Lock up the river Thames. Its members are partly elected by users of the port and partly appointed by the Secretaries of State for Defence and the Environment, Trinity House, the Greater London Council and the City Corporation. The P.L.A. has its own police but there is also a river police division of the Metropolitan Police. The Thames-side Consultative Committee of officers comprises G.L.C. planning and highways officers, planning officers of the sixteen London Boroughs past which the Thames flows, representatives of the Thames Advisory Committee of the London Tourist Board, commercial interests and the P.L.A. After consultation with the London Boroughs Committee, there was constituted a committee of three G.L.C. members and a representative from each of the sixteen riparian boroughs. The Thames-side Consultative Committee of officers reports to this

Committee and its objects include preservation and improvement of the docks and riverside trade and of the amenities of the river.

A Covent Garden Market Authority was established in 1962 and a Lea Valley Regional Park Authority has been constituted by statute.

RENT OFFICERS

The Rent Acts 1965–68 gave security of tenure to the tenants of all dwelling-houses with a value of £400 or less in Greater London (£200 or less elsewhere). In general, a landlord cannot evict a tenant without first obtaining an order from the local county court. These provisions are of great social significance and, following the disclosures in the Milner Holland Report, penalties are provided for harassment of tenants. The penalties for unlawful eviction and harassment were increased by the Criminal Justice Act, 1972. In some areas Tenancy Relations Officers have been appointed.

Rent officers began to function in Greater London in 1966. The functions of the rent officers relate solely to the regulation of fair rents of unfurnished accommodation in dwelling-houses with a rateable value of £400 or less (with certain limited exceptions). All except personal circumstances are to be taken into account in determining fair rents; thus the age, character, locality and state of repair of a dwelling-house are all relevant. Scarcity value is to be disregarded, so that the number of persons seeking accommodation in a particular neighbourhood is to be ignored. The town clerks of the thirty-two L.B.C.s carried out their statutory duty, cast upon them individually, to appoint rent officers, who cannot be dismissed without the consent of the Secretary of State. The Treasury pays the salaries of rent officers. Thus, although rent officers were appointed by the town clerks, they are not local government officers. The rent officers are of a high calibre and some are former local government officers; their efficiency and integrity have been commended in Parliament.

Applications to rent officers fall into two categories:

1 To fix a fair rent by means of registration;
2 To issue a certificate of fair rent.

Applications to fix a fair rent may be made by a landlord, by a tenant, or jointly. The certificate procedure is useful where conversion of an old house into flats or a new block of flats to let is envisaged. The rent officers have no power to inspect premises or to compel answers, since the essence of their work is informality.

It has been considered appropriate to describe this aspect of the operation of the Rent Act in Greater London at this juncture. It should be emphasized, however, that the Act applies to the country as a whole. Accordingly, rent officers and Rent Assessment Committees have been appointed in other areas of the country, including Birmingham, Bristol, Manchester, Yorkshire, Scotland and Wales. The procedure under the Housing Rents and Subsidies Act, 1975, relating to the revision of rents of certain council house tenants, has been outlined in Chapter 3. The 1975 Act requires local housing authorities to consult the local Presidents of Rent Assessment Panels in this respect.

FURTHER READING

Jackson, W. E.: *Achievement – A Short History of the L.C.C.* (Longmans).

Mitchell, R. J., and Leys, M. D. R.: *History of London Life* (Penguin, 1968).

Harrison: *A History of the Working Men's College 1854–1954* (Routledge and Kegan Paul).

Royal Commission on Local Government in Greater London 1957–60 (Cmnd. 1164, H.M.S.O.).

London Government: Proposals for Reorganization (Cmnd. 1562, H.M.S.O., 1961).

London Government: the London Boroughs (H.M.S.O., 1962).

Ruck, S. K.: *London Government and the Welfare Services* (Routledge and Kegan Paul, 1963).

Bater and Young: *The Hornsey Plan* (Association of Neighbourhood Councils, 1971).

Society of Town Clerks: *Local Government Reorganization – Recent Experience* (S.T.C., 1972).

Wistrich, E.: *The First Years of Camden* (London Borough of Camden, 1972).

London Boroughs Management Services Unit: *Annual Report, 1973/74.*

London Facts and Figures, Greater London Council, 1974.

Blackham, Col. Robert J.: *London For Ever the Sovereign City* (Sampson, Low).

Questions

1. What were the composition, structure and functions of the Metropolitan Board of Works and the London County Council?
2. What reasons led to the establishment of the G.L.C.? What are the justifications for its creation (if any)?
3. Why was it thought necessary in 1963 to reorganize London government?
4. Describe the functions of the London Borough Councils and the Corporation City of London. How have they been affected by the Local Government Act, 1972, the Water Act, 1973, and the National Health Service Reorganization Act, 1973?

10 SCOTLAND

Historical introduction

The pattern of local government in Scotland in the nineteenth century was based on the burghs (towns), the counties and the parishes. The Local Government (Scotland) Act, 1889, built on this structure by providing that local government services were administered by these authorities on an elective basis. A modified structure was created under the Local Government (Scotland) Act, 1929, based on the four cities of Edinburgh, Glasgow, Aberdeen and Dundee; 21 large burghs, 176 small burghs, 33 counties and 196 districts. The four large cities were the equivalent of the English county boroughs and thus exercised all the functions of local government in Scotland. The larger burghs exercised most functions except education and valuation for rating. Scottish county councils administered most functions in the landward or rural areas, with some delegation to district councils; they also exercised some functions on behalf of the burghs. County and burgh councils were responsible for housing, public health, rate collection, refuse disposal and street lighting. District councils administered certain minor functions (e.g. promotion of recreational facilities) and some services delegated to them by the county councils. Anomalies abounded in this pattern and a large burgh with a much greater population than a small county council could have had a more restricted range of functions.

It was against this background that a White Paper, *The Modernization of Local Government in Scotland* (H.M.S.O., Cmnd. 2067) was published in 1963, followed by the *Report of the Royal Commission on Local Government in Scotland* (the Wheatley Report, 1966–69, H.M.S.O., Cmnd. 4150) which recommended a two-tier structure of seven regional and thirty-seven district authorities and changes in functions, management, relations with government departments and the role of councillors. After consultations a White Paper, *Reform of Local Government in Scotland* (H.M.S.O., Cmnd. 4583), appeared in February 1971, at the same time as the English White Paper and the Welsh Consultative Document. Another period of consultation followed and the Local Government (Scotland) Bill was introduced by the Secretary of State for Scotland in November 1972. It received the Royal Assent on 25 October 1973; the first elections for the new regional, islands and district councils were held in May 1974 and all powers, functions and duties vested in the new authorities on 16 May 1975.

Structure functions and elections

The Act creates nine regional councils, three islands councils and fifty-three district councils. Thus there are nine regions instead of the seven originally proposed and separate status has been conferred on the Orkney, Shetland and Western Isles. The four great cities cease to be all-purpose authorities and, with their surrounding areas, now constitute district authorities within the regions in which they are situate. The huge Strathclyde Region covers a population of over 2½m but its boundaries correspond broadly to a distinctive area with regional characteristics and large-scale problems. According to the Scottish Office Brief on Local Government Reform issued by the Reference Unit of the Scottish Information Office (November 1973), any sub-division would have meant a weakening of administrative cohesion and an impairment of strategic opportunities. Strong authorities are being created at both levels which should attract to the public service both elected members and permanent officials. The Local Government Boundary Commission for Scotland is making an initial review of administrative and electoral boundaries and will subsequently make comprehensive reports in ten- to fifteen-year cycles. The pre-existing twenty police forces have been reduced to eight. The Act provides for change of name subject to the approval of the Secretary of State. County names can still be used for postal purposes. A table of functions is set out below.

Functions

Regional and islands authorities:

Strategic planning	Harbours
Industrial development*	Water
Roads	Flood prevention
Public transport	Coast protection
Road safety	Sewerage
Airports	Tourism*
Ferries	Countryside*
Parks*	Food standards and labelling
Recreation*	Registration of births, deaths and marriages
Police	Electoral registration
Fire	

Education
Youth employment
Social work
Consumer protection
Weights and measures
Valuation
Museums*
Art galleries*
Community centres*

District and islands authorities:

Local planning†
Development control†
Comprehensive urban redevelopment†
Building control†
Listed Buildings†
Conservation areas†
Housing
Rents
Derelict land*
Tourism*
Countryside*
Caravan sites
Recreation*
Parks*
Museums*
Libraries†
Community centres*
Art galleries*
Environmental health
Cleansing
Refuse collection and disposal
Public conveniences
Markets and slaughterhouses
Burial and cremation
Food hygiene
Clean air
Inspection of shops, offices and factories
Licensing: liquor, betting and gaming, theatres and cinemas, dogs

* Exercised concurrently by regional and district authorities
† Except in Highlands, South West and Border regions, where the function will be regional.

District and islands councils may draw up schemes for community councils after full public consultations, preparation of plans for the proposed areas and of codes of procedure and arrangements for elections.

The schemes must be approved by the Secretary of State, who may hold a public inquiry to consider objections or representations and he may amend a scheme. Community residents may then petition the district or islands council to cause an election to be held and set up a community council. This procedure is unlikely to be invoked before 1976. Community councils will be able to raise funds, receive grants and help from the larger authorities. Community areas may be based on a village or small town with its hinterland or on urban divisions but the aim is to provide a ready base to gather views and decisions on local action. It will be interesting, in due course, to compare the progress and development of the community concept in Scotland and in Wales; and to compare and contrast it with the amended system of parish administration in England.

Simultaneous elections were held on 7 May 1974, for the new regional, islands and district councils. Every region and islands area has been divided into electoral divisions and every district into wards. Each district and ward returns one councillor. The newly elected councils undertook preparatory work until 16 May 1975 when the pre-existing authorities disappeared. The scheme of the Act is that the normal term of office will be four years but the first two terms of office for district councillors will be of three years each. Thus future elections for district councils will be held in 1977, 1980, 1984, 1988, and so on; and future elections for regional and islands councils will be held in 1978, 1982, 1986, and so on.

Finance

Until 1974, rates were determined and levied by each county, in respect of the landward area, and by each burgh. Authorities providing services other than those provided by the rating authority requisitioned for a share of the cost on the rating authority. The county requisition for major services usually accounted for the larger part of the burgh rate. Under the 1973 Act, every new Scottish local authority will determine a rate for its own services but the regional and islands authorities are now responsible for rate collection and administration. The system of requisitioning has now largely disappeared. A new rate rebate scheme has been introduced extending relief higher up the income scale and closely modelled on the rent rebate provisions of the Housing (Financial Provisions) (Scotland) Act, 1972. 90 per cent of the cost will be met by the government. Valuation functions are assigned to regional and islands councils; and the next general revaluation of property has been postponed until 1978, after which revaluation should be quinquennial.

The Act continues the rate support grant system, except that, as in England and Wales, grant orders are now made annually instead of biennially. The Act also provides for the making of contributions by the outgoing authorities to the initial expenses of their successors during the period from May 1974 to May 1975.

All the new local authorities must have a general fund, must arrange for the proper administration of their financial affairs and maintain accounts subject to audit. The Secretary of State may approve capital expenses on a programme basis. The Commission for Local Authority Accounts in Scotland now arranges for the audit of all local authority accounts, either by accountants in professional practice or by auditors in its own employment. The Commission considers their reports, investigates matters raised and makes recom-

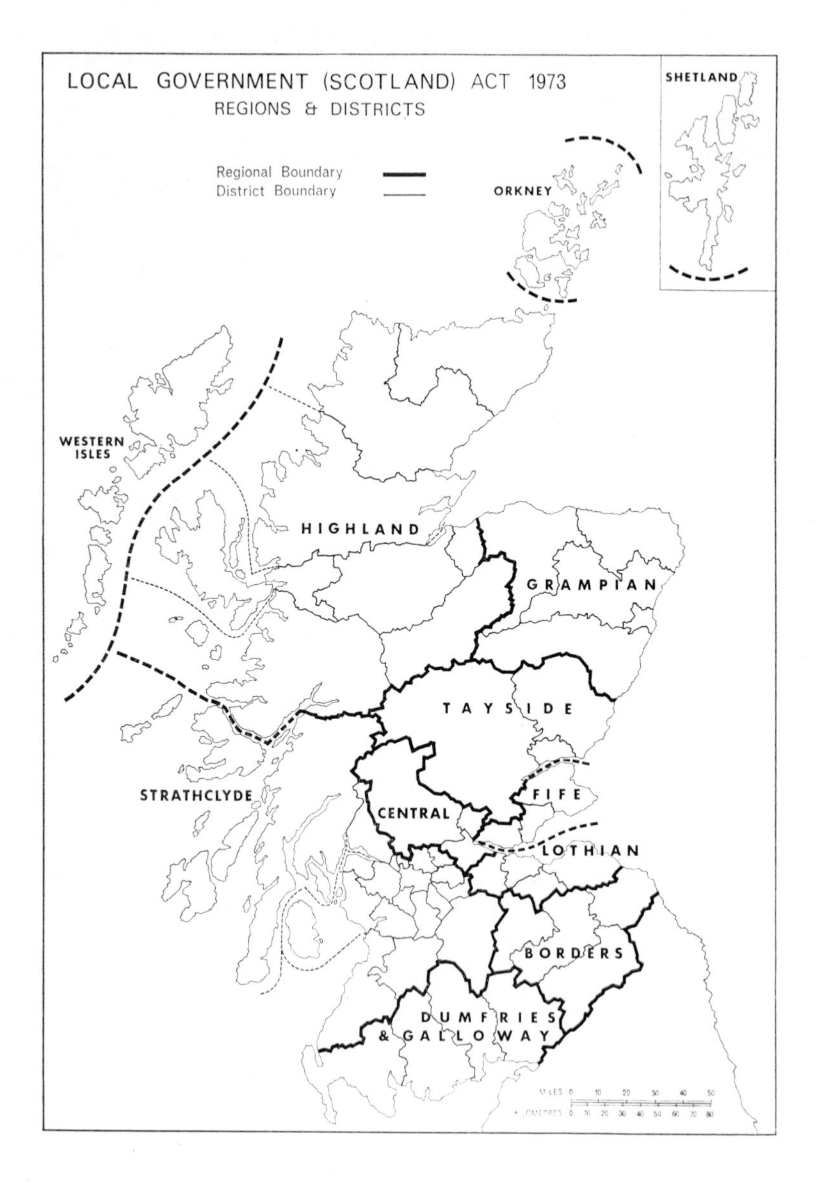

Fig. 6 Local Government (Scotland) Act, 1973, Boundaries of Regions and Districts

9 Regions and 53 Districts

Note: Figures in brackets denote the number of districts in each region

Borders Region (4)
- Tweeddale
- Ettrick and Lauderdale
- Roxburgh
- Berwickshire

Central Region (3)
- Clackmannan
- Stirling
- Falkirk

Dumfries and Galloway Region (4)
- Merrick
- Stewartry
- Nithsdale
- Annandale and Eskdale

Fife Region (3)
- Kirkcaldy
- North East Fife
- Dunfermline

Grampian Region (5)
- Moray
- Banff and Buchan
- Gordon
- City of Aberdeen
- Kincardine and Deeside

Highland Region (8)
- Caithness
- Sutherland
- Ross and Cromarty
- Skye and Lochalsh
- Lochaber
- Inverness
- Badenoch and Strathspey
- Nairn

Lothian Region (4)
- West Lothian
- City of Edinburgh
- Midlothian
- East Lothian

Strathclyde Region (19)
- Argyll
- Dumbarton
- City of Glasgow
- Clydebank
- Bearsden and Milngavie
- Bishopbriggs and Kirkintilloch
- Cumbernauld
- Monklands
- Motherwell
- Hamilton
- East Kilbride
- Eastwood
- Lanark
- Renfrew
- Inverclyde
- Cunninghame
- Kilmarnock and Loudoun
- Kyle and Carrick
- Cumnock and Doon Valley

Tayside Region (3)
- Angus
- City of Dundee
- Perth and Kinross

3 Islands Authorities
- Orkney
- Shetland
- Western Isles

mendations to the Secretary of State and the local authorities. These new provisions are designed to enhance the public accountability of local authorities and to reduce the function of the Secretary of State in this sphere. Where the Commission recommends recovery of any amount, the Secretary of State receives any representations made by persons affected before deciding whether or not recovery should be made in full or in part.

Central control

The Secretary of State for Scotland is the Cabinet Minister responsible for Scottish affairs and the Scottish Office is located in Edinburgh and Whitehall. In 1973 the Secretary of State completed a comprehensive review of statutory controls exercised by his Department over local authorities and a number of relaxations were incorporated in the Act. He is given a general power to make Orders modifying or revoking controls over local authorities contained in existing legislation without having to introduce an amending statute. England followed Scotland in this respect as a similar provision appears in the Local Government Act, 1974, dealing mainly with finance. In Scotland, control of capital expenditure on a 'programme' basis has replaced the old system of controls over individual borrowing applications. Under previous legislation a local authority needed the consent of the Secretary of State to spend money up to a limit in the interests of the area or its inhabitants or for certain charitable or other purposes. The 1973 Act removes the need for consent and raises the limit from the equivalent of a rate of 8p to 2p in the £.

Other examples can be culled from the fields of planning and transport. Thus, in relation to factory building, consent is no longer required for the erection of buildings or carrying out of constructional or other works on land. Similarly, most ministerial controls over P.T.A.s have disappeared and all controls over P.T.E.s are now exercised by the regional authorities. The only important exceptions in the first case relate to orders designating a passenger transport area, transfer of existing municipal bus undertakings to a P.T.E., bus licensing and control of local rail services.

Management, staffing and related matters

The New Scottish Local Authorities, Organization and Management Structures (the Paterson Report, 27 September 1973) recommends the corporate approach to management and closely follows the Bains recommendations in England. The report was produced by a

Working Group appointed by the four Scottish local authority associations. The high level of skill and experience of many councillors and officials is commended in the Paterson Report and the tribute already paid in Chapter 7 to their English and Welsh counterparts can be applied with equal strength to Scotland. Nevertheless shortcomings in the pre-existing system were pinpointed in the Paterson Report. Examples given of lack of co-ordination were housing developments without community facilities; education and housing provisions out of place with each other; and social work problems caused by unilateral action. The Report urged new authorities to be wide ranging in assessing community needs and to look beyond the immediate confines of an individual service or a single year's estimates.

The Paterson Report recommended the establishment of a policy resources committee to provide co-ordinated guidance on policies, priorities, resource allocation and major programmes; appointment of a chief executive; creation of a management team of chief officers led by the chief executive; and adoption of a unified system of policy planning. The Report stresses the need to preserve public contact and to avoid remoteness or bureaucracy, advocating extensive decentralization of regional services. Particular stress is laid on the need for the 'one-door' approach for the convenience of members of the public, thus echoing the sentiments of the Seebohm Report on Local Authority Social Services which led to the statutory reorganization of the social services.

A Scottish Local Government Staff Commission was established in April 1973 to review recruitment and transfer of staff and generally to advise the Secretary of State. The Secretary of State has power to give directions to local authorities or joint committees to implement the Commission's advice.

Taxable attendance allowances payable as of right replace loss of earnings allowances for councillors. A complaints machinery is envisaged with the appointment by the Crown of a full-time independent Commissioner for Local Administration. From May 1975, committees of local authorities shall admit press and public except where they exclude the public for good reason (e.g. appointment of staff or approval of contracts).

A Property Commission advises on identification of property to be transferred covering both functional and common good property, the former including schools and police stations. Property held on common good funds of existing burghs will go to the district authorities, who must have regard to the interests of the inhabitants of the former burghs, except in the case of the four city districts, where regard is to be had to the interests of all the people of the new area. Presumably new local authority associations will be formed based on the regions, islands and districts.

Tradition and dignities

As far as possible, local rights, dignities and customs should be preserved under the new structure, if desired. Powers of local authorities to make by-laws for good rule and government are unchanged but the Secretary of State for Scotland is now the confirming authority for all by-laws made under local Acts. Accordingly, the Sheriff's power to confirm by-laws is abolished.

The right of the burghs to reward notable service by enrolment as honorary freemen is inherited by district and islands councils. Building control is transferred from Dean of Guild Courts to district councils but Deans of Guild may be co-opted to building committees. Parts of burghal charters will be inoperative and certain property and common good rights now pass to the new district authorities. The influence of Roman Law can be discerned here in the development of Scots Law. However, if a charter's provisions are not in conflict with the 1973 Act and still apply to a particular group, they can remain in force.

The chairmen of the new districts incorporating Edinburgh, Glasgow, Aberdeen and Dundee are Lords Provost and Lords-Lieutenant. The Queen may appoint Lords-Lieutenant and lieutenants in regions and islands areas; and lieutenants in the districts. Transitional provisions apply to pre-existing appointments.

FURTHER READING

White Paper; *Modernization of Local Government in Scotland* (H.M.S.O., Cmnd. 2067, 1963).

Royal Commission on Local Government in Scotland 1966–69 (the Wheatley Report, H.M.S.O., Cmnd. 4150, 1969: £2.)

White Paper: *Reform of Local Government in Scotland* (H.M.S.O., Cmnd. 4583, 1971: 22½p).

Scottish Development Department Report (H.M.S.O., Cmnd. 5274, 1972: 90p).

The New Scottish Local Authorities, Organization and Management Structures (the Paterson Report, 1973) 85p.

Scottish Office Brief on Local Government Reform (Reference list – Scottish Information Office, St Andrew's House, Edinburgh, EH1 3DQ).

Questions

1. What criteria would you use in estimating the success of town and country planning within the area of either a city district or a district in Scotland?
2. 'A reasonable measure of financial independence is an essential element in local democracy.' Discuss this statement with particular reference to the way local government is financed in Scotland.
3. Do you think that the establishment of regional authorities in Scotland is justified? Will the new regional authorities promote effective and efficient local government?
4. What reasons had Parliament for the establishment of separate islands authorities in the Local Government (Scotland) Act, 1973?

GENERAL READING: PART TWO

Hart, W. O., and Garner, J. F.: *Local Government Law and Administration* (Butterworth, 1973).

Cross, C. A.: *Principles of Local Government Law* (Sweet & Maxwell, 1974).

Golding, L.: *Teach Yourself Local Government* (English University Press, 1975).

Jennings: *Principles of Local Government Law* (University of London Press, 1960).

Alan Stewart: *Them at the Council* (the Stewart Report, A Kind of Epitaph).

Siddall: *Life in a Mayor's Nest* (Bell).

INDEX

Printed in Great Britain by
Cox & Wyman Limited
London, Fakenham and Reading

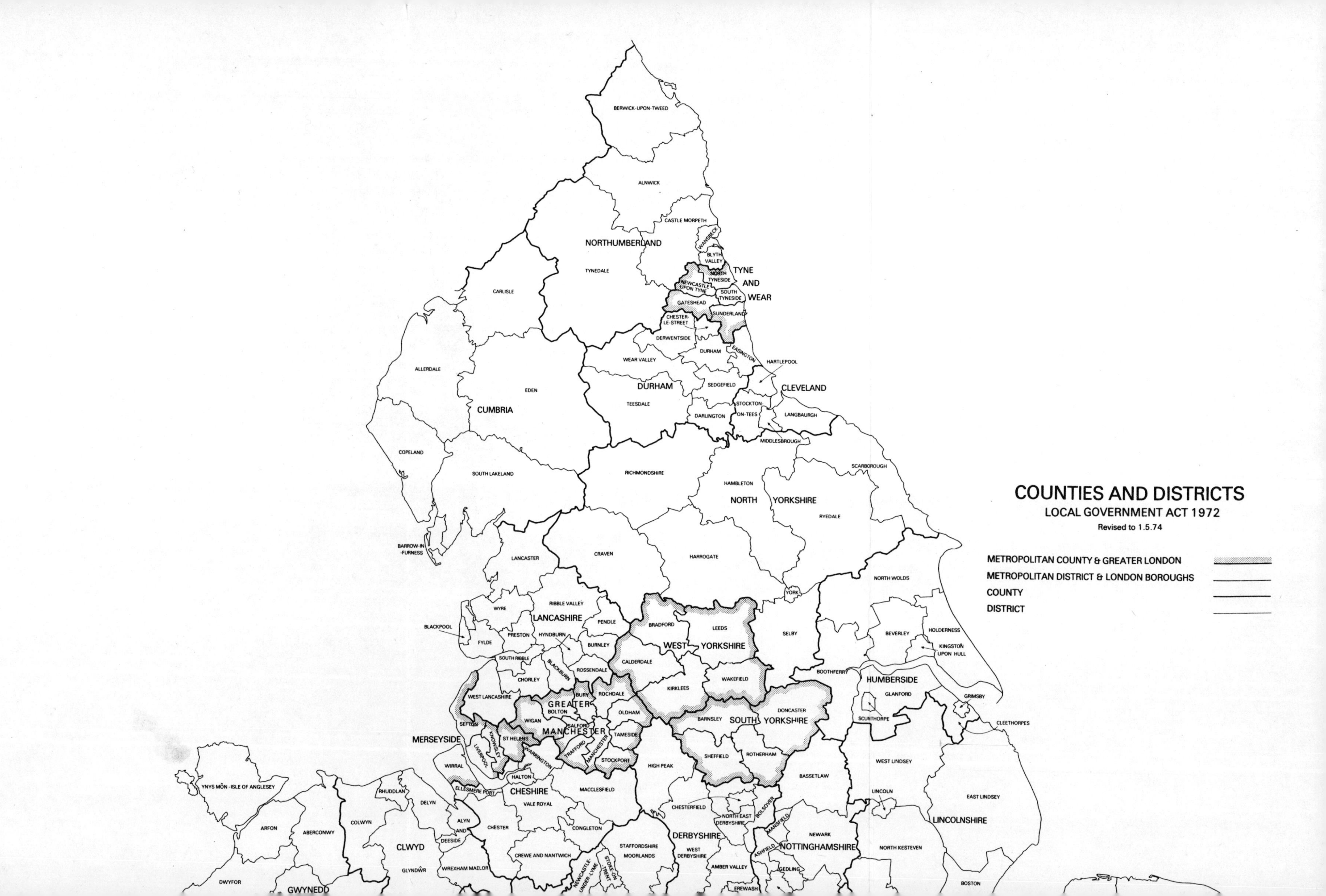

COUNTIES AND DISTRICTS
LOCAL GOVERNMENT ACT 1972
Revised to 1.5.74
METROPOLITAN COUNTY & GREATER LONDON
METROPOLITAN DISTRICT & LONDON BOROUGHS
COUNTY
DISTRICT
BERWICK-UPON-TWEED
ALNWICK
CASTLE MORPETH
NORTHUMBERLAND
WANSBECK
BLYTH VALLEY
TYNEDALE
NORTH TYNESIDE
TYNE AND WEAR
NEWCASTLE UPON TYNE
SOUTH TYNESIDE
GATESHEAD
SUNDERLAND
CARLISLE
CHESTER-LE-STREET
DERWENTSIDE
EASINGTON
DURHAM
WEAR VALLEY
HARTLEPOOL
ALLERDALE
EDEN
SEDGEFIELD
CLEVELAND
CUMBRIA
TEESDALE
STOCKTON-ON-TEES
DARLINGTON
LANGBAURGH
MIDDLESBROUGH
COPELAND
SOUTH LAKELAND
RICHMONDSHIRE
SCARBOROUGH
HAMBLETON
NORTH YORKSHIRE
RYEDALE
BARROW-IN-FURNESS
LANCASTER
CRAVEN
HARROGATE
NORTH WOLDS
YORK
RIBBLE VALLEY
WYRE
LANCASHIRE
BLACKPOOL
PENDLE
BRADFORD
LEEDS
SELBY
BEVERLEY
HOLDERNESS
FYLDE
PRESTON
HYNDBURN
BURNLEY
WEST YORKSHIRE
KINGSTON UPON HULL
SOUTH RIBBLE
BLACKBURN
CALDERDALE
ROSSENDALE
BOOTHFERRY
HUMBERSIDE
CHORLEY
KIRKLEES
WAKEFIELD
GLANFORD
GRIMSBY
WEST LANCASHIRE
BURY
ROCHDALE
DONCASTER
GREATER MANCHESTER
BOLTON
OLDHAM
SEFTON
WIGAN
SALFORD
BARNSLEY
SOUTH YORKSHIRE
SCUNTHORPE
CLEETHORPES
MERSEYSIDE
KNOWSLEY
ST HELENS
TAMESIDE
LIVERPOOL
WARRINGTON
TRAFFORD
MANCHESTER
SHEFFIELD
ROTHERHAM
WEST LINDSEY
STOCKPORT
WIRRAL
HIGH PEAK
BASSETLAW
HALTON
YNYS MÔN - ISLE OF ANGLESEY
RHUDDLAN
ELLESMERE PORT
CHESHIRE
MACCLESFIELD
LINCOLN
EAST LINDSEY
DELYN
VALE ROYAL
CHESTERFIELD
NORTH EAST DERBYSHIRE
BOLSOVER
ALYN AND DEESIDE
COLWYN
LINCOLNSHIRE
ARFON
ABERCONWY
CHESTER
CONGLETON
MANSFIELD
NEWARK
DERBYSHIRE
STAFFORDSHIRE MOORLANDS
CLWYD
ASHFIELD
NOTTINGHAMSHIRE
NORTH KESTEVEN
CREWE AND NANTWICH
WEST DERBYSHIRE
NEWCASTLE-UNDER-LYME
STOKE ON TRENT
GLYNDŴR
WREXHAM MAELOR
AMBER VALLEY
GEDLING
DWYFOR
GWYNEDD
EREWASH
BOSTON